'In the 21st century, theology might appear to be some historical residue left over from out-of-date worldviews, and studying it as quirky as trying to decipher Egyptian hieroglyphics – but less interesting. Stephen Cherry characteristically makes us think again, pointing to theology as the disciplined, human and holistic way in which we explore the eternal questions that hover over every century. The rumour of God that circles the book, implying that reality might be worthy of trust, is compelling and unignorable. I hope this work will entice a new generation of theologians fit for purpose, imaginative in language, engagement and prayer.'

– Canon Mark Oakley, Chancellor of St Paul's Cathedral

'In a world of glib sound-bites, a world that sneers at "experts", it has never been more important to encourage people to read and think for themselves. Stephen Cherry's accessible, passionate and entertaining introduction to the key ideas of Christian theology does just that. Vital ideas are explained lucidly and powerfully, old ideas are brought to life in new contexts, and Stephen Cherry not only makes the case for theology, but stimulates a new enthusiasm for it.'

– Malcolm Guite, Priest, Poet, and Chaplain
of Girton College, Cambridge

'This is an unusual and original book designed to interest and encourage those thinking of studying theology or religious studies as an academic discipline – more specifically, those thinking of reading it at university. Unlike many academic subjects, Cherry argues, theology is more a matter of the questions you ask, than any traditional certainties: "as an enterprise [it] only makes sense if you know that you don't know all the answers already". Supporting his thesis by a sweeping history of Christianity in 20 tweets, the Dean of King's College, Cambridge, gives an interesting and thoughtful introduction to a subject that has increasingly come to fascinate him the more he has studied it.'

— *Stephen Prickett, Regius Professor Emeritus of English, University of Glasgow, and Honorary Professor, University of Kent at Canterbury*

GOD-CURIOUS

EXPLORING ETERNAL QUESTIONS

STEPHEN CHERRY

Jessica Kingsley *Publishers*
London and Philadelphia

First published in 2017
by Jessica Kingsley Publishers
73 Collier Street
London N1 9BE, UK
and
400 Market Street, Suite 400
Philadelphia, PA 19106, USA

www.jkp.com

Library of Congress Cataloging in Publication Data
A CIP catalog record for this book is available from the Library of Congress

British Library Cataloguing in Publication Data
A CIP catalogue record for this book is available from the British Library

ISBN 978 1 78592 199 5
eISBN 978 1 78450 473 1

Printed and bound in the United States

'I have no special talents.
I am only passionately curious.'
Albert Einstein

'I have no special talents.
I am only passionately curious.'

Albert Einstein

CONTENTS

WELCOME

This little book is a personal invitation to explore theology. I sat down to write it in the hope that it would helpful to people who are considering what to read at university. But as the writing continued, I came to feel it could be intriguing to people at any stage of life. Theology is such a huge and hugely interesting subject.

Actually theology is much more than a 'subject'. It's more like a form of seeking, a quest; and that is why for me theology is not so much about answers, as about questions; not so much about knowing, as about wondering; not so much about gaining knowledge, as about enriching your perspective on experiences that make you wonder.

In universities today the subject of theology is being challenged and reshaped, but the quest of theology is much older than any of our educational institutions. It is a seeking after wisdom that is based on the intuition that there is more to life than we can ever know. I suspect that such seeking is as old as language itself – or at least as old as the capacity to ask questions about the meaning and purpose of life, and to wonder about what might be just beyond the realms of our ordinary experience and common sense.

One way to 'define' theology might be as the quest to understand God. However, in the tradition to which the book seeks to introduce you, such a quest is deeply intertwined with the quest to understand other people and the quest to understand yourself; three projects that are integrated in the ancient religious teaching that you should love God, love your neighbour and love yourself.

Theology is something you will enjoy if you find yourself asking questions like these: 'Why are we here?', 'What might become of us in the very long-term future?', 'Why do some very good people have to endure very painful experiences?', 'Does the word "God" have meaning?', 'To what extent are religions similar or different?', 'Are human beings born bad or are they fundamentally good?', 'Why are special books so important in many religions?', 'What do religious traditions have to teach us about justice or truth, peace or hope?', 'Is "love" merely a romantic phase of life, or does it lie at the heart of the deepest reality?' If questions like these resonate with you, if they matter to you more than the easy, trivial or glib answers they often get, then you might well enjoy exploring theology.

Theology, then, is the discipline of asking the best possible question about the most important matter that you can imagine. It is about coming to the limit of your own knowledge and insight and posing the question, 'What is beyond?'

And if that intrigues you, do read on.

CHAPTER 1

CONFESSIONS OF A RELUCTANT THEOLOGIAN

Let me begin by telling the story of how I came to be a theologian of sorts.

When I was at school I loved science. I felt that Biology and Chemistry in particular were teaching me extraordinary truths about the world and at times I felt like my mind would explode with new knowledge. I also liked the way scientists found things out – by making observations and doing experiments. I decided to continue with science at university. I did very badly in my A-levels but still got into a good university to study what was then called 'General Science'. I knew I was going to a completely new world. No member of my family had been to university before, and I was very anxious about it. In fact I felt that I had only got in because of an administrative error. Today I would say that I had a bad dose of 'imposter syndrome', but I had never heard of that in those days so I just suffered from it in sad ignorance of the reality that many people feel the same way in a new environment – that they don't deserve to be there, or don't belong. And it was in the middle of my worst episode of imposter syndrome that I was asked by the Dean of Sciences which *particular* sciences I would like to study. I answered 'Biology and Chemistry' and to my horror received the answer, 'But you are not very good at those subjects – why not try something else?'

Although genuinely shocked by the honesty of the comment, I soon recovered my composure because the idea of trying something else was very attractive to me. In truth, I was delighted because during my last year at school I had discovered, by reading and listening to radio programmes, that there was a subject about which I had not heard at school called 'psychology' (this was in the 1970s – today everyone has heard of psychology, and rightly so because it's a great subject). At that time I felt that the scientific study of behaviour would be the most interesting and fascinating subject imaginable. So I signed up for Psychology, and in my first year studied it along with Plant Science (or Botany as it used to be called) with a little Anthropology thrown in. A year later I had done very well in my first-year exams and transferred to single honours Psychology. Two years after that I had got a good enough degree to be able to move to another university to do a PhD.

Before telling you how that worked out I want to go back to my school days because my fascination with science and my love of it was a complete mirror image of the way I engaged with English and History. They didn't do anything for me at all. And as far as I was concerned the time spent studying Religious Education (RE) was, despite what I now recognize as the valiant efforts of my teachers to make it relevant, deeply disappointing. For one reason or another I didn't connect with these subjects and it didn't seem to me to be at all likely that anyone could become any wiser by working in these areas. This was a little odd because I was at the time an enthusiastic member of a local church and found services meaningful and moving. Moreover I remember that while still a teenager I had the thought that the church and the school – which were at opposite ends of the small town where I lived – represented different sorts of wisdom. That might strike you as a curious thing to think, but in some ways it reflects a very ancient distinction, and suggests that there are different kinds of knowledge and different criteria for judging what is true.

While still at school I discovered the library in the nearest big city and read a book called *Saint Francis, Nature Mystic* which I am sure I didn't fully understand but the impact of the book, among other factors no doubt, was to make me think about the natural world in a completely different way to the science of biology.[1] Then I took out a book called *I and Thou* by Martin Buber, a profound Jewish thinker, and Paul Tillich's *The Courage to Be*, which I recall not reading – though I browsed through it several times, and the title made be think and ponder and wonder.[2] I remember trying to discuss Buber's ideas about the difference between education and propaganda in a Chemistry lesson. I can't think why it seemed relevant, but it's no wonder I didn't do very well in my A-level exams. My mind was on other things. I was fascinated by science, but more deeply concerned to learn wisdom.

Now – to return to the post-graduate part of the story... While I was very proud to get a place to do research for a PhD in psychology it didn't turn out as well as everyone had hoped. In fact, I never finished it. I feel ashamed about that now, as I think the project was worthwhile and I would have learnt a lot by completing it. What happened during it, however, was a parallel to what happened during my A-levels. That is, I began to become more interested in the pursuit of wisdom than with things that I was meant to be focusing on. While

---

1   Edward A. Armstrong, *Saint Francis, Nature Mystic: The Derivation and Significance of the Nature Stories in the Franciscan Legend* (Los Angeles, University of California Press, 1973).

2   Martin Buber, *I and Thou* (New York, Scribner's, 1958); Paul Tillich, *The Courage to Be* (London, Fontana, 1964).

the research project I was engaged in was fascinating – I was asking whether and how the way in which people understand their own minds impacts on the way in which they learn – the actual process of organizing experiments and analysing the data left me intellectually cold.

Meanwhile, the idea that had developed in my mind while I was still in school that I should devote myself to God's work as a priest in the church got stronger. I went through the selection process and after a year as a teacher of O- and A-level Psychology found myself at a theological college – an institution where people prepare to be clergy, often now called 'vicar school' – in Cambridge and, somewhat against my will, was signed up for another degree, this time in Theology.

I wasn't optimistic. Those trying-so-hard-to-be-relevant but ultimately unconvincing school RE lessons were still a strong memory, and the compulsory challenge of learning Greek struck me as being just as dull as analysing data. I felt that I had gone out of the empirical frying pan into the linguistic fire. Nor did Biblical Studies promise to float my boat. No one seemed to be asking the questions that really mattered. No one seemed to be getting down to matters of life and death and meaning and purpose. St Francis and Martin Buber had set my sights on an intellectual world where people would think and write and talk about matters that made a profound difference to the way in which lives were lived, and relationships developed. After all, I thought, if God is God then surely there must be awe and wonder and amazement in the way in which people who believe in God approach their studies. Surely, I argued with myself (and anyone else who would listen), if a subject is called 'Theology' it really ought to be eternally fascinating and the participants must be passionate about what they are saying.

Then one day I had an intellectual conversion experience. It was in a lecture on a fourth-century bishop and theologian from North Africa called Augustine, and in particular about a book

he wrote called *Confessions*.[3] I had not come across it before, despite the fact that it is one of the most significant books in the history of the Western world. As I heard about it in lectures, and as I started to read it, I realized that this, at last, was the subject that I had long been looking for. Theology was actually about issues that mattered deeply and that were well beyond the reach of science.

In *Confessions* Augustine puts in front of the reader his struggles to work out what he really believes about the things that matter. As you read it you get a real sense of getting close to someone who is wrestling not with personal problems but with some of the fundamental issues that face all human beings – about identity and certainty and what to trust and so on. He also discusses at length some issues that still puzzle people today – such as how memory works and what time is. On the subject of time he says that he seems to know exactly what it is until he starts to think about it: a comment that is still often repeated in books about time written today.

He is also very interested in God – and what it might and might not be true to say about God. And like any good theologian he is concerned about the negative side of life – what is evil, where does it comes from, is it real, will it last? What I hadn't really spotted at the time was that the whole of the book is a prayer – that is, it is addressed to God. So there is something spiritually as well as psychologically intimate about it. It is what you might call soul-writing. It is certainly not a dry-as-dust essay, and yet in it Augustine is racking his brains as hard as he can to think things though.

As you can tell, I was hooked. Augustine is one of the great theologians to whom I will introduce you later in this

---

3   The edition of Augustine's *Confessions* that everyone was reading in those days was that by R.S. Pine-Coffin, published by Penguin Classics, but the most recommended version today is Henry Chadwick's translation published by Oxford University Press, 1991.

book. So too is the man who was teaching that course, Rowan Williams, who went on to become Archbishop of Canterbury and is now back in Cambridge. One of the great things about both Rowan and Augustine is that they seem to be interested in everything. I can't detect any real outer limit to their thought, but at the same time they seem able to penetrate very deeply into the issues that they focus on. I found this very impressive and extremely attractive as I sat in those lectures and thought about them afterwards, and it was this experience of being taught about Augustine by Rowan that drew me to theology and to realize that at last I had found my intellectual home. I hadn't turned my back on what science had to teach us or the concerns of psychology, but I had found a different framework in which to think about things, one that seemed to have no outer boundaries and where, I discovered as I listened to Rowan explain Augustine, you discover a kind of kinship with people who lived very many centuries ago – because they too were thinking about some of the matters that I was, in an immature but nonetheless earnest way, thinking about.

But there was more to the degree course than Augustine. Another aspect that I found completely fascinating was the study of other faiths under the heading 'Self and Salvation'. It was that experience that convinced me that the best way to study faith today, the best way to be a theologian, is not to huddle in a corner with people like me but to try to connect with people *unlike* me. To do this you have to be reasonably clear about what you are like, what your core beliefs and identity are, what your story is. You need some kind of base, but, in my experience, it is by encountering religious and theological difference and challenge that you can genuinely grow as a theologian – and as a person. That's why I believe that Theology and Religious Studies should go together and not be separated out. It's great to encounter the superstars of your own tradition, but important to listen and listen and listen to those who see things completely differently, whether very close relations or extremely different cousins.

While doing my theology degree I also took the opportunity to write a dissertation, and for this I turned not to one of the great historical figures or controversies but to one of the Latin American 'liberation theologians'. These theologians take the view that theology begins not with high-sounding, abstract statements or with the intense study of scriptures, but with the conditions of the poor and oppressed. They believe that it is theology's task to help them to describe the truth of their lives and to achieve freedom or liberation. It was a very different approach to that of Augustine, but the key theological concerns are central in both. What really matters to people? What is evil? Can things change? What can we do about it? What might divine action look like in this situation? Given this reality, how can we speak of God? What might God's perspective on this be?

After I graduated I moved to a suburban part of Manchester to serve as a curate, taking church services, visiting the sick and conducting lots of weddings and baptisms and funerals. I had a young family and we were at least 200 miles from our nearest relations and to top it all after about 18 months I contracted glandular fever and rubella at exactly the same time. I was in a state of perma-exhaustion for weeks and perhaps because of this my mind returned to some of the theological questions that naturally emerged from the sort of ministry I had been engaged in. I also realized that although I had been quite a serious student of theology there were many areas in which my education was a little bit thin. It was also about this time that the big question that framed my intellectual life for the next couple of decades began to take shape in my mind. The question was, 'How does the forgiveness of God relate to the forgiveness that human beings may or may not extend to each other?'

These factors, coupled with the feeling that it would be really fun to have a job working among students, took me back to Cambridge. Although I was busy in term time, I had more freedom in the vacations and was able to work for a PhD on the theology of forgiveness. I successfully completed that in 1995, by which time I was back in parish ministry, this time as a vicar in a multicultural and multireligious part of a town in the Midlands. I enjoyed very much the challenge of relating to people of other faiths such as Hinduism, Sikhism and Islam as well as getting to know what people found attractive in neo-Pagan movements like Druidry. In fact, I found the environment of the Council of Faiths, of which I was chair for a few years, to be one of the more lively theological environments I have ever been in. It wasn't that everyone was a scholar, though some definitely were. It was that people were fascinated by the whys and wherefores of each other's beliefs, values and practices, and that we were all quite uninhibited in our questions and observations because there was a good ethos of mutual respect.

Today I am Dean of King's College, Cambridge. This means that I am responsible for the life of its world-renowned chapel. I am also Director of Studies in Theology, Religion and Philosophy of Religion at King's College. I do a lot of administrative work, take a lot of services, care for people as best I can, but I am also continuing the theological quest that I started while still at school. I am searching for wisdom by reading widely, thinking deeply, questioning relentlessly, and through travel and by being hospitable at home, meeting and talking with people who see things differently.

So, as I offer you this personal introduction to theology, I do so as someone who preferred science at school, but didn't do too well at A-level; someone who explored psychology at university, but became disenchanted with the empirical approach; someone who loves the stimulation and challenge of people of other faiths and their ideas, but usually goes home from such discussions feeling not only a deep respect for what I have heard but also more convinced than ever of the merits of a Christian approach; and someone who is not a full-time or career academic, but who has blended pastoral, administrative and educational work together over the years while remaining convinced that engaging with the study of theology is fascinating, fun and of real importance.

It is both inevitable and obvious that I am taking a Christian approach but, as you can see, I believe that openness to other traditions, curiosity about what other people believe and a respect for people for whom the idea of faith is either deeply unattractive or makes no sense at all, are fundamental aspects of what it means to be a theologian. Without those ingredients it seems to me that theology is self-stunting and ultimately self-defeating. You just can't be a theologian and feel so certain about things that you expect never to get a big intellectual surprise or positive emotional shock as you read other people's views or meet people from different traditions.

Other people would introduce you to theology differently, but if you would like a personal introduction I can only give you mine. If you have an inkling that I might be an interesting guide, then do read on.

CHAPTER 2

IN THE BEGINNING

Imagine a small group of early humans getting by as a community of hunter-gatherers. On the whole they are minding their own business and not asking each other any questions apart from merely functional ones, such as where shall we find sticks, how can we light a fire, can we eat those berries and might that be a deer that we could catch and eat hiding behind those trees? Then, one day, a leading member of the community is killed during a hunting expedition. Rather than just leave the body where it is someone suggests that the community should gather around it, maybe cry or shout out some feelings to the skies and then do something that both disposes of the body and expresses the community's sense of loss. Later the same day a child asks her mother a question about where that person is now. The mother gives a shrug of the shoulders which doesn't satisfy the child at all. Nor is she happy with the idea that the person is in the corpse. So she keeps asking questions and tries to make sense out of the different answers the adults give.

A year later this child is running through the woods when she trips and falls and breaks an arm. She is in great pain and cannot look after herself or do what the other children are doing. Brooding away the hours on her own she feels angry and asks, 'Why did this happen to me?' and 'What's the point of me when all I can do is feel pain and listen to stories?' This bright child then starts to make up her stories. Stories that don't exactly answer her questions, though they do make it easier to live with them. As she shares her stories, other members of the group talk with her about them and some begin to adapt them. A young man one day tells her about the stories that come into his mind when he sees an animal killed, or when he is especially hungry or when he is walking in the dark and looking at the lights in the sky. They start to talk about the edges of life, and start to develop ideas about what is beyond it. They enjoy doing this very much and after a while it becomes a custom to do this at nightfall and at sunrise. They make up more stories to tell but soon they realize that they don't need more stories, but they do need to enjoy the old ones even more and to tell them in different ways, turning some of them into poems or songs and, after they have told them, sharing in a bout of shared laughter or crying or silence.

There are different ways of thinking about the scene I have just painted. One would be to see this as a myth about the origins of religion, and one thing that happens when people study theology is that they study religion. We will come to that question a bit later, but for now I want to suggest that the two main characters in our story represent the first theologians on the planet. And I call them this not because they invented a religion but because they asked questions that stretched the boundaries of their imaginative world. But actually they did more than this – they not only asked the questions but they also asked the questions out loud and discussed them with each other.

And this, I believe, is what lies at the heart and core of theology: putting the deep, often unanswerable, eternal questions that occur to us, often at significant or difficult times of life, out there into the open and seeing what other people think or believe about them, and how they try to answer them, and what difference their answers make.

This elemental reflectiveness began to take a different form, and assume a different level of significance, when human beings developed a sense that they were not alone in the universe and didn't have to rely on their own thinking to work out the answers to the most important questions. This is where God came in, so to speak. Quite who or what God is, and how God 'came in' are *theological* questions.

Some people take the view that God waited to reveal who he or she or it was until people were able to understand this revelation. Others take the view that God was always there, is always there, seeking, as it were, to be noticed, but that it is only from time to time that human beings are able to detect God's presence. Some take the view that God doesn't exist and so any sense of God is just make-believe. Atheism is an important reality for theologians to consider today, as is the often-related view that science is the *only* reliable method for finding out what is true, and that therefore only scientists are genuinely and seriously interested in distinguishing truth from falsehood – everything else being a 'matter of opinion' or 'subjective'.

Theologians are in fact just as concerned as anyone else to work out what is true and what is nonsense. It just so happens that they are doing it in an area not only where there is legitimate debate, but also where there is a *very long history* of debate and disputation, and where no one clear method has ever been agreed. So there are perhaps two main differences between science and theology. The first is subject matter, and the second is lack of an agreed method in theology.

There is one theological method, however, that is rather like science, and that is 'negative theology', or in the Greek word that is often used to refer to it, *apophatic* theology. This is the method of identifying things that it is unhelpful, inappropriate or wrong to say about God. It can be thought of as a way of scraping away the nonsense that has gathered around the idea of God over the years. As I have mentioned, one of my own areas of study is that of forgiveness. A friend of mine who became interested in forgiveness not for any academic reason, but because her sister was murdered and she had to work out how to respond, has a very interesting and powerful phrase about forgiveness, and the words associated with it like 'confession', 'sin', repentance' and 'grace' – all important theological words with rich meanings and implications for how people understand intimate and important aspects of their lives. She describes forgiveness as being 'barnacled with centuries of religious convictions'.[1] What Marian Partington is getting at here is that the meaning of the word, especially to a person faced with the huge challenge of knowing how to relate to someone who has seriously harmed them or someone they love, is sadly not revealed by the way in which religious people have talked about it over the years. Rather it is hidden, encrusted over, buried and submerged by year after year of, to use a phrase that I learnt from a wise old priest who died years ago, 'pious clap-trap'.

To my mind this is a shameful state of affairs. The last thing religion or theology should be about is obscuring the truth, or making wisdom inaccessible. But there is no denying that this happens or that there is, to use a metaphor, a lot of noise that obscures the beautiful music that might just be at the core of any religion. Some of this noise is generated from within the religion and some is projected on it from outside.

This means that there is a genuine theological task to identify and name and push to one side the nonsense, the noise and

1   Marian Partington, *If You Sit Very Still: A Sister's Fierce Engagement with Traumatic Loss* (London, Jessica Kingsley Publishers, 2016), p.66.

the barnacles that all too easily get connected up with religious truth. It may sound odd at first, but part of the task of theology is to identify things that people of any particular faith do not or should not believe. This is as important, one might say, again speaking metaphorically, as making sure that the floor of the milking parlour is kept clean despite the fact that cows are notoriously, spectacularly and regularly incontinent. You may not have expected me to say that a main task of a theologian is to identify and sweep away theological BS – but that is exactly what I am saying, and it is exactly what theologians do and have done. And, if I may make a generalization, they tend to go about this aspect of their work with great energy and passion.

This has not always been good. There have been times in the past where disputes within the church were not only conducted with energy but with the threat of expulsion for those who believed or taught the wrong things. The word 'anathema' means 'damned' or 'cursed', and it has a long history, going back to the earliest recorded writings of the Hebrew people. There is obviously a danger of intolerance creeping in once people get the hang of *anathematizing* those they disagree with, or who present an unpopular minority view. And just because you have been subject to an anathema doesn't mean that you can't anathema back. Once you get into those sorts of cycles it soon gets out of hand, and a war of words where people aren't listening to each other is only ever a small step from a war of physical violence.

The dangers of anathematizing people should not distract us from the important task of cleaning the floor of the theological milking parlour, by identifying beliefs that might seem to be coherent but which are in fact nonsense, and sweeping them out. One intriguing book lists over 100 'Christian disbeliefs', among them: 'that God's being is the effect of something else'; 'that God's being is not innately relational'; 'any notion of more than one God'; 'that the right of any one of us to occupy our unique time and space is something we ever have to justify'.[2]

The full list gives a hint of the range of things that theologians are concerned with – and they are obviously much, much wider than the nature of God. The question of what it means to be human, and what human fulfillment looks like, the question of what sense we are to make of the created world – the universe even – and what is going on at the limits of life and death and in the aftermath of cataclysmic events – all this is food and drink to a theologian. But it is not a *carte blanche* to make up your own opinion in isolated ignorance. Rather it is an invitation to engage seriously with a community of people who today, and down the ages, have tried to make sense of the mysteries that beset thoughtful human beings.

If you find any of this intriguing please read on…

---

2   Christopher Morse, *Not Every Spirit: A Dogmatics of Christian Disbelief*, 2nd edition (London, Continuum, 2009).

CHAPTER 3

WHY ENGAGE WITH THEOLOGY?

The short answer is because it is fascinating, fun and important.

However, before I explain why that is the case it might be worth dealing with a few of the reasons why people might think it is *not* worth studying theology.

FIVE NOT VERY GOOD REASONS FOR NOT ENGAGING WITH THEOLOGY

The first reason that might be suggested is this: *I don't believe in God therefore I can't possibly study God.*

If theology were limited to questions about the nature of God then you might have a point. That which doesn't exist can't have a nature… However, theology and religion have been important in history and philosophy. They continue to impact hugely on current affairs and inform the ways in which people respond to realities as different as beauty and tragedy. In other words, what goes on when people are motivated by religious faith and theological conviction is a matter of significance well beyond the community of believers. Indeed, an atheist may feel that theology is too important a subject to be left to those who believe in God. And certainly, faith and religion aren't going to go away just because atheists are dismissive of believers.

The second reason is the opposite of the first. *I not only believe in God but I know God very well, and for this reason I don't want to study God any more than I would want to study my parents or my partner.*

I agree that if you are completely confident that you know all there is to know about God then theology is not for you. Theology is only worth exploring if you think that other people's views about God are at least as interesting as your own.

The third reason why you may not want to study theology is because you think *it is not a real subject of study but just a professional training programme for ministers of religion.*

It is true that this used to be the case, and that there are places where people study theology only for this reason. It is also true that if you study theology at university you may well come across people who are studying for this reason, and you will almost certainly read books by people who are trained and ordained ministers and you may well be taught by some. But theology stopped being the province of the clergy alone a long time ago, and it has become a much more lively subject since – so don't let that one worry you.

The fourth reason you may not wish to study theology is because *it's just about learning what the Bible says or what people of different religions do.*

If you think this you may be muddling up theology, the most exciting subject imaginable, with what has all too often passed for 'religious education' at school, which is all too often dominated not by the pursuit of life's deepest questions but by learning superficial details about religious traditions.

The fifth reason is a bit like the fourth in that you may think that theology *is entirely concerned with ancient and irrelevant philosophical problems of the 'How many angels can dance on a pin-head?' variety.*

I can guarantee that you won't be discussing that question, or anything like it, if you engage with theology today! The agenda has moved on. Theologians today seek to learn from the past and to understand why theologians of previous eras posed and answered certain questions in the way they did, but they also seek to learn from theologians of other faiths and to respond to the problems and predicaments that occur in today's world as well as to the classic questions such as the existence of God and the consequences of believing specific doctrines.

THREE VERY POSITIVE REASONS FOR EXPLORING THEOLOGY

IT'S FASCINATING

We have already considered the range of questions that theologians consider, but it's worth noting that today the study of theology almost always involves encounters between people who see the world very differently, have quite different religious practices and sometimes very different values. It is certainly not limited to people who believe in God, or even to those who think that being religious or spiritual is a sensible option for a human being. On the other hand, if you study theology you are likely to come across, either in person or though their writing, people of deep faith who take their own religion very seriously both as a practitioner and as a thinker.

Theology is fascinating even at the simply human level. It's extraordinary that people can hold such different convictions and yet get on really well. And at the same time it's very odd that people can hold very similar views and yet get into serious and bloody conflict over what seem to be rather minor differences to anyone outside their tradition.

One of the things that I have found interesting as I have recently re-read some of the great theologians of the Reformation era, is just how extremely *rude* they are to each other, and how confident they are that they themselves are right. What Martin Luther had to say to Desiderius Erasmus would make anyone blush! It is also extraordinary that people with religious convictions have put such huge amounts of energy into their controversies. It is said of Augustine (the one who wrote *Confessions*) that he worked hard all day as a bishop and then worked all night as a theologian, writing books and commentaries and letters. Sometimes he was in a reflective mode, wondering about who he was and what his life meant, sometimes he was in dispute with those who understood human nature quite differently, sometimes he was sketching out (I mean writing thousands of words about) his understanding of how society should be organized.

One of the things that people easily forget when they think about theology is that people have often been prepared to die for it, that theological opinions have often been a matter of life and death. There are different versions of this. Some people will die for their faith because they believe that martyrdom is a fast track to paradise. But this isn't the driver of most martyrdom down the ages and is not, in a Christian understanding, true martyrdom. A martyr is a witness and true martyrs are those who have been so committed to their faith, their understanding of the truth, that *witnessing* to this truth became more important to them than their own life. True martyrs don't want to die, but they are not prepared to lie their way out of a situation when matters of ultimate truth are at stake. True martyrdom is not about seeking any personal reward but about standing up for truth, however costly that proves to be.

Along with the idea of martyrs goes the idea of *heretics*. Although people don't often make this point, it almost goes without saying that all heretics are theologians. They are people who have thought things through for themselves and come to conclusions that religious authorities have not found acceptable. A heretic is not someone who suddenly has a dodgy idea in their head. A heretic is someone who has taken a lot of trouble to come to their unpopular view and is prepared to take the flak for maintaining their position. The study of theology involves the study of heresy and heretics. And thank goodness for that, because it is potential 'heretics' who push the boundaries and possibilities of theology wider and wider. The pursuit of deep wisdom involves the possibility of making major mistakes. It may seem strange, but to a theologian that is all part of the pursuit of the truth. It is fair to say that, just as some mistakes in life are worse than others, so some errors in theology are worse than others and it is therefore possible to think of heresy as sometimes very negative; it does not follow that all heresy is bad or that all those branded as heretics have been in error or done a disservice to the truth. Often, inevitably enough, heretics are castigated not because they are actually and ultimately wrong, but because what they have to say is inconvenient and awkward for the powers-that-be.

Heretics are often people with great insights and ideas as well as strong-mindedness and courage who just happened to lose the dispute at the time. Quite how that dispute looks with several hundred years of hindsight is one of the questions a theologian might ask. And any theologian who has a lively and independent cast of mind might end up a heretic today. The penalty for being a heretic is no longer to be burnt at the stake, any more than the penalty for being orthodox in your faith might lead to being fed to the lions. But theology is a subject where the stakes can be high, as it is so much more than a dry intellectual matter. This is part of what makes it a fascinating and compelling, not to say, once you get started, a *compulsive* business. Indeed, I prefer to call it a pursuit or a quest because one of the great things about theology is that you never have to stop, because there is always another theological question to be asked and, possibly, answered.

IT'S FUN

Theology is fun partly because it is one of the most interdisciplinary of subjects. To study it properly you have to engage with philosophy, history, anthropology, psychology and sociology. But that's not all. Recognizing that people express religious, spiritual and theological ideas indirectly, theology very often involves the study of literature. Novels, poetry and drama often include or allude to theological themes and discussions. Theologians also try to progress their understanding by looking at historic works of art. The pictures, buildings and music of religious communities can teach us a great deal about their beliefs and values, and in today's world you are as likely to find theological questions addressed in films as you are anywhere else. So yes, theologians go to the movies and try to 'read' or interpret them in a theological way.

Words are important in religion and theology, but they are rarely the last word – because one of the things theologians are interested in is what people have to say about matters that can't be adequately expressed in words. Indeed, theologians are very interested in the limits of knowledge, just as they are interested in the limits of life, and what may be beyond knowledge and experience. Theology is the subject for you if you are interested in the 'something more' to life that no one can see. This is often referred to as the 'transcendent'. Part of the fun of theology is that we can never be 100 per cent sure that we, or anyone else, are right about the transcendent, and so there is always room for another point of view. And yet no theologian is content to shrug their shoulders and say, 'Nobody knows, so it's not worth thinking about.' Rather, a theologian will say that although no one knows, and no one will ever know for certain, it is really important to give the matter deep thought and extended consideration.

One of the observations that I have made in life, not least in my ministry as a pastor, is that many people will be happy letting life go by, enjoying the good times and not asking many questions until something goes seriously wrong for them or someone they love. It's for this reason that theology is often born out of suffering or catastrophe. Good, interesting, lively compelling theology doesn't often grow on happy trees in jolly gardens. It tends to spring up from the ruins of some kind of lost hope or shattered vision or, if not that, then some genuine puzzlement and dissatisfaction with existing answers. Theology never grows out of smugness, but comes out of perplexity and the need to find answers to questions that keep us awake at night or which occur to us when life (or death) stops us in our tracks.

Maybe that idea doesn't quite belong under the heading of theology as fun, but there is in fact a kind of fun to be had in looking difficulty and despair in the face and letting that reality challenge complacent and easy believing. And there is a huge amount of fun to be had (though 'fun' is too light a word now – joy would be better) in seeing hope rise again in the once despairing, in seeing the liberation of the oppressed, the forgiveness of those who have made great mistakes and the reconciliation of sworn enemies. No theologian would claim that the study of theology will make these things happen, but for theology to be complete it must be interested in the upside of life, even if it often begins in the downside.

To study theology is to have permission to think about things that are above and beyond our normal capacities. If you like everything cut and dried then theology will be no fun for you at all. If you think that all perplexity, suffering and sadness can be brushed under the carpet then theology is certainly not for you. Theology wants and needs all this stuff to be in full view on the table. This is one reason why some people of intense and clear faith find theology so difficult. But if you think the idea of starting on an intellectual adventure that has no limits and could last for the rest of your life – then theology is your kind of fun.

Theology can be fun in a deeper way than this when it puts *everything* in the context of the possibility of God and casts all human striving, questioning, suffering and aspiring into the cloudy mist of an overcast sky which *may* go on for ever, but which may clear away and reveal God's eternal timespan, God's glorious omnipotence, God's perfect peace, God's profound joy and God's endless love. This is theology lived not in the *certainty* that God will make everything good but with the possibility held open that God not only exists but might be able to transform even the worst of experiences. We may not be aware of that much of the time, but even to have a hint of it when consumed by our own earthbound troubles and murky self-obsessions can draw from us a raised eyebrow, a smile or an infectious laugh: all signs that there is yet fun to be had, and that joy still lives.

One of the things I remember most clearly about the hours that I spent when, as a newly ordained curate, I was on call as a hospital chaplain and regularly sat in the company of those who were near death, often together with their most intimate companions, was how often there was a shared moment of laughter. This was never unkind or irreverent, and rarely sought or contrived. But often enough a slight quirk of shared perception, something said or seen, or perhaps overheard from somewhere else in the hospital ward which in this situation was not annoyingly incongruous but amusingly so, parted the clouds and let in a shaft of sunlight which told us, truthfully and amusingly and soberingly, that ultimately we are all in this together and that we are not alone.

When considered theologically, joy, like love, is to do with human connection that is more than human. It's about a solidary and fellowship that sees us all united at the deepest level of who we are. In a remarkably rich theological book a Filipino priest, Benigno Beltran, reflects on his experiences over 30 years living with the 25,000 scavengers on the famous 'Smokey Mountain' garbage heap in Manila. As I read it I was surprised that Beltran repeatedly returned to the reality of fun and laughter in the midst of the squalor, stink and disease of the dump. He writes of the *joyousness* of scavengers that is intrinsically connected to their belief. He believes that this joy in the midst of suffering and squalor challenges disbelief and agnosticism. He then refers to science writer John Horgan who suggests that agnostics and atheists should be as troubled by the problem of the good things of life, listing 'friendship, love, beauty, truth, humor, compassion, and fun', as believers are by the problem of natural evil. 'Never forget the problem of fun,' he writes.[1] It is good advice for any theologian, though as yet I have never seen the subject on a degree syllabus.

What these people are getting at is the inadequacy of *reductionism* as an explanation for what matters in human life. Reductionism is the view that there is *nothing more* than basic ingredients; it is the view that the whole is *not* more than the sum of the parts. As Benigno Beltran puts it, 'To view the world in purely physical terms is inadequate to explain the religious experience of the people of Smokey Mountain. It does not do justice to the way they understand their humanity. For the scavengers, religious experiences are critical for their explanation of what being human means and their understanding of personhood.'[2] His point is that reductionism or materialism not only squeeze the meaning out of life, they also drain it of the fun and joy that there is to be had – even on Smokey Mountain.

---

1   Quoted in Benigno P. Beltran, *Faith and Struggle on Smokey Mountain: Hope for a Planet in Peril* (Maryknoll, NY, Orbis Books, 2012), p.100.

2   Beltran, *Faith and Struggle on Smokey Mountain*, p.101.

IT'S IMPORTANT

Third, theology is important. There was a time not very long ago when it was common for people to think that religion would die out. There was a time not very long ago when it was common for people to think that religion would die out. Some might assume that this was a feature of the public response to war – either in the 1920s or the 1950s and 1960s. However, its roots are found in the nineteenth century.

In 1882 the philosopher Friedrich Nietzsche declared that 'God is dead' (adding that 'we have killed him'). Previously, in 1867, one of the big-name English literati of the Victorian era, Matthew Arnold, wrote a poem called 'Dover Beach' in which he referred to 'the long withdrawing roar of the sea of faith'. Arnold was connected with the strong-minded and eminent Victorian Leslie Stephen, whose father and grandfather were leading evangelical clergy, very much involved in social campaigns such as anti-slavery. They were members of the so-called Clapham Sect alongside social reformers like William Wilberforce and John Newton (the former slave-ship captain who wrote the hymn 'Amazing Grace') and missionaries such as Henry and John Venn.

As the twentieth century dawned the advance of atheism continued. Thomas Hardy wrote a poem called 'God's Funeral' between 1908 and 1910, and the First World War put an end to any easy idea that 'God is in his heaven and all is right with the world.' This was the era in which Leslie Stephen's daughters, Virginia Woolf and Vanessa Bell, found themselves at the heart of an elite London group that was as different as it is possible to be to the Clapham Sect of their grandparents. This was the 'Bloomsbury Group', which was famous for its artistic and progressive values. After the First World War religious authority figures were no longer as trusted as they had been and it became increasingly common for people to think that what was taught or thought about God was essentially what people *made up* about God. This approach was given a huge boost by the work of Sigmund Freud who developed the idea that the human mind was dominated by thought processes of which we were not aware, and that 'God' was essentially an idea conjured up in the recesses of our 'unconscious' to help us feel better and cope with life's more difficult challenges.

But the end of faith wasn't only prophesied by philosophers, poets and psychologists. Sociologists came up with the idea of 'secularization' almost as soon as their subject was invented. Studying the number of people who attended church from year to year, they soon saw that the numbers were declining and, plotting graphs of the decline, proved to their own satisfaction that church-going should be over and done with by the early years of this century. The sociologists were both right and wrong. Church-going has declined in many places, especially in the north of England, but there are also places where it has increased, and the actual ultimate decline of religion, the death not only of God, of which Nietzsche spoke, but of believing in God, has not yet happened. In fact, the reverse is the case. The spin doctors of the 'New Labour' government of Tony Blair famously announced in 2003 that they didn't 'do God'. But that didn't matter: plenty of other people were busy doing God, although the equally 'new atheists' were becoming increasingly vociferous, annoyed perhaps that their predecessors had not managed to put an end to faith and that, if anything, the tide of the sea of faith seemed to have turned and was coming back in again.

There are many reasons for this, and not all of them are based on the better aspects of religious thought and practice, but that's not the point. The point is that religious beliefs and religious organizations are today having an enormous impact on the lives of people all over the world. Religion has not died out and it isn't going to die out any time soon. It had a very serious wobble in Europe and Britain, but the edifice of organized religion has not toppled, and the whole new phenomenon of people calling themselves 'spiritual but not religious' has exploded. This is evidence of 'faith', the sort of thing that a theologian ought to try to understand. And if you have the cast of mind that is theological you may be thinking, 'Hmmm, there is interesting and important stuff here. I wonder whether anyone understands all this. Let me try to find out.'

And you will want to read on.

CHAPTER 4

JESUS OF NAZARETH AND RICHARD DAWKINS

Let me make a suggestion that you *may* find strange. Here it is: among other things, Jesus of Nazareth was a theologian. Now, let me justify it. It seems to me from what I read in the Bible that he certainly thought very deeply about what mattered and how people should live. Early in his life he went out of his way to understand the religion of his family and people. For example, he got lost when he was young because he was so keen to learn from the elders in the Jerusalem Temple. When he was a young man he went on a tough spiritual retreat to work things out in his heart and mind. This was his 40 days and 40 nights in the wilderness, which may have been intended as a long sojourn with God but it became a head-to-head tussle with the devil, which, ultimately, Jesus won.

After this he set off on a mission in which he told people his new teaching, healed people and, as people understood it at the time, cast out many demons. But he also engaged in conversation with other people who were asking deep and difficult questions, and took time out to be on his own, thinking and praying and thereby preparing himself for the challenges to come.

It seems that at some point Jesus must have come to the conclusion that the religion of his people was not being practised in the right way. He came to the view that it often lacked sincerity and depth and that people far too often prioritized performing religious rituals over pursuing social justice or caring for the poor. In a word, he felt that his people misunderstood the nature of God and the implications of believing in God.

Needless to say this didn't go down at all well with the religious authorities, and Jesus got into great trouble when he took his mission to Jerusalem. The rest, as they say, is history – which doesn't mean that we know exactly what happened, but that people have been talking about it ever since. And 'talking' in the broadest sense: gossiping, writing books, arguing, turning it into literature and plays and films, celebrating with rituals, using it as the basis for new songs and great musical compositions, seeing whether it might help make sense of the idea of God or establish that there is no God, and all the while trying to do two rather important things: on the one hand, to work out whether this is sensible or wise or true or in some other sense meaningful, and, on the other hand, to use it to try to make sense of the questions that pop up unbidden in our minds, which we don't know how to answer. Questions which, in fact, we are not sure that we can share with anyone else because we fear that even to ask these questions is a sign of madness.

Which might be a good moment at which to introduce Professor Richard Dawkins into the discussion, because he is of the view that religious belief is a sign of madness and that God is a delusion.

Dawkins is a paradoxical figure. He doesn't believe in God, but he does think that religion can be a good thing, and is supportive of the place that the chapel, choir and clergy have in his Oxford college. On the other hand, he is not at all keen on the study of theology and wrote in a letter to the *Independent* newspaper in 2007 that there was no longer a good reason for including theology as a university subject.

One could argue it quite differently and say that if Dawkins is right and that religion is madness and God a delusion then there is *every* reason to make a study of religion and to try to understand why human beings have been and remain so very persistent in holding onto their absurd religious beliefs. There are many atheists in contemporary society, but one of the interesting things about some of them is that they often behave rather like enthusiastically religious people of an earlier generation. They write lots of books saying, 'I am right and you are wrong' – religious people often do that. They seek to have an influence on the way people mark the transitional points of life – birth, death and the making of committed relationships – another feature of religious activity. They concern themselves with questions of how to live a good life, and are interested in human 'flourishing'. Some metropolitan atheists even gather themselves as a kind of church in order to pursue their atheistic version of theology and religion, basing their gatherings on most of the ingredients you would expect at an evangelical church service – apart from the confession of sins or, as one journalist put it, 'a recognition that we are anything less than super'.[1]

So perhaps it is sensible to ask the question who is madder – those who behave in a religious way because they believe in God, or those who behave in a religious way because they *don't* believe in God? That too is an interesting and very contemporary theological question – and as such it is a matter for discussion; there is no cut and dried, black and white or scientific answer.

The truth is that dogmatic certainty, although a trait of some religious and God-believing people, is a trait that can also be

---

[1] Andrew Watts, 'The church of self-worship: Sunday morning with the atheists', *Spectator*, 22 February 2014.

found elsewhere in the human community. What matters about it from the perspective that we are exploring at the moment is that, while dogmatism and certainty *look* like theology, they are (in my view) the *opposite* of theology because they represent the refusal to listen to a new and different set of questions, answers or stories, and that is a contradiction of the fundamental drive of theology which is to *understand better*. It is only when people are open to different questions, answers and stories, and to working hard to grasp their significance and importance, as well as whether they can be considered to be objectively true, that they can be a participant in the enterprise called theology.

This little book explores what it is like to engage with theology today, which is why the emphasis is on not being dogmatic but being open to others and sharing in a conversation that has been going on since the dawn of human questioning. As we have already noted, many people who hold especially fervent religious beliefs find theology a very difficult and uncongenial subject. In fact, theology as an enterprise only makes sense if you know that you don't know all the answers already.

Professor Frances Young has recently expressed this in the following way in a book which reviews the theology of the early Christian centuries and connects it with the sort of questions and concerns that people have today. This area of early theology is often known as 'patristics' as it involves studying the work of the early theologians who are traditionally known as the Church Fathers, and the word for 'father' in both Greek and Latin, the languages they used, is 'pater'.

It is in the context of exploring patristics that Young asks whether the power of scientific explanation can lead us to the conclusion that there is nothing that stands outside science. Comparing Richard Dawkins with Charles Darwin, she finds that the Victorian scientist's approach is not unlike that of the early church theologians she has spent her life studying.

Darwin's uncertainties about God were rubbed home by a certain humility of mind, reinforced by his own theories... Darwin, unlike Dawkins, was agnostic rather than aggressively atheist. An element of agnosticism is an appropriate theological stance, since creatures, deeply integrated into the created order and limited by their creatureliness, can hardly know all there is to know.[2]

She goes on to say that 'a degree of agnosticism is characteristic of the church fathers, who consistently affirmed the otherness of God, recognizing that infinity, or lack of definition, necessarily implied inability to grasp such a Being'.[3]

One of the things that I like about Frances Young as a theologian is that she is honest about who she is, the way in which her mind has changed over the years and what she cares about as she writes. And so she is insistent in the book from which these quotations come (a serious 500-pager published by Cambridge University Press) that she is only interested in theology that stands up given her experience as a carer of her disabled son, Arthur, who is now in his forties. Indeed she has written a (significantly shorter) book which focuses on the theological issues that disability raises, based on her personal experience.[4]

To do justice to theology you have to have a bit of agnosticism about you, you have to know that there is much you don't know, and you also need to have a good deal of curiosity. If you feel that's you, do read on.

---

2   Frances Young, *God's Presence: A Contemporary Recapitulation of Early Christianity* (Cambridge, Cambridge University Press, 2013), p.65.

3   Young, *God's Presence*, p.65.

4   Frances Young, *Arthur's Call: A Journey of Faith in the Face of Severe Learning Disability* (London, SPCK, 2014).

CHAPTER 5

THE ANTIDOTE TO FUNDAMENTALISM

RELIGIOUS STUDIES

If you look carefully at what departments of theology offer in British universities you will often find that they include 'religious studies' or 'the study of religion' in their titles. Some just add the word 'religion' to the word 'theology'. On the other hand, if you take a look at theology in the United States you will find a clearer distinction between the institutions that offer theology and those that focus on religious studies.

One way of thinking about the difference between theology and religious studies is that theology tends to look at things close up and religious studies looks at things from a distance. You could imagine the theologian looking down a microscope while a professor of religious studies uses binoculars to survey the religious landscape. Both are necessary, and both can be fascinating, fun and important. Indeed you would be wise if you didn't get all your information and insights from people who look into microscopes all day, but then again you would be

43

wise if you did pay attention if someone said, 'I know it looks like that from a distance but from close up you see things very differently.' Think in terms of biology and the advances of the last 50 years. If Watson and Crick had not looked at things in very great detail DNA would never have been discovered. But if we didn't have people considering things from a distance we would have no sense of the complexity of the ecosystem or the importance of ecology.

To use another metaphor you might say that theology should never take place in an intellectual vacuum but that it needs a number of 'philosophical friends' if it is going to be a healthy, valuable and worthwhile enterprise. Among these philosophical friends I would list religious studies, philosophy, history and literature. In this chapter we will consider history and literature, and then give philosophy, the closest and perhaps most argumentative of friends, a chapter of its own.

HISTORY

History is important for theology in two ways. First, since it is only relatively recently that it became generally understood that belief is primarily a private matter, the impact of religion on historical affairs is greater than a contemporary person may at first appreciate. This means that the impact of religion, and the theology that is caught up with religion, on political affairs historically has been huge. This is so whether you are thinking about great affairs of state, or the way we educate children or deal with those who break the law, or how we care for the sick, or whatever. Religious sensibilities in our day are often focused on issues around the end or beginning of life, the legitimacy of conflict and the organization of human sexuality. Concern with justice or international development and the peaceful reconciliation of conflict have recently been getting more and, in my view, well-deserved attention. The media would have you think that the management of sexuality is the most important thing to religious people, especially Christians. This is complete nonsense. It just so happens that we are going though a time of rapid social transition in this area, and because religion is attractive to people who like tradition and find change difficult, the church is having great difficulty not with sexuality itself but with the pace of social change. (Well, that's part of the story; I think that there is a more complicated story to be told about religious attitudes to sex and sexuality, but in what I have just written I am emphasizing a side of the story that is rarely remarked upon.)

Wide-ranging as these contemporary concerns are, a study of history will soon teach you that the idea that there are separate things, 'religion' and 'politics', is not an assumption that people have always made. Jesus may have hinted at it when he said, 'Render to Caesar the things that are Caesar's and to God the things that are God's' (Matthew 22.21) but he was speaking as a rabbi and so part of his message was, 'The way you relate to the emperor, and indeed to money, is all a matter of religious concern.' And it is therefore, we might add, something that a theologian might be expected to think carefully about with a view to developing some informed and wise opinions.

The second way in which history is of concern is when it comes to understanding theological arguments and statements from the past. There is never an intellectual vacuum and there is never a social or historical vacuum. In order to understand why someone said *this* or believed *that* or thought it was outrageous that someone else was sure that something else was correct, you need to know something about what was going on at the time. And what was going on at the time is either 'history', if it was a long time ago, or 'current affairs', if it is now. In a later chapter I offer a 'history of theology in fewer than 20 tweets'. In order to make that work I have needed to offer a little commentary on each tweet. That, in a way, is an example of historical theology

– putting things in the context that allows us to understand what is being said and why. History is vital for theology.

LITERATURE

Literature is important for theology too. A student of theology can expect to read a lot of theological books and essays, but the study of theology will be terribly limited if this is the only material that theologians read. Poetry has been important for theology since the very first scriptures were written. The book of Psalms in the Bible is a collection of 150 poems of different types. Some are based on accepted and stated theological positions. Others work more like little theological exercises, as the poet seems to be trying to work something out. Psalm 137 is a good example. The poet is deeply troubled to see that bad people are often successful and as the psalm goes on, expresses the problem, expresses feelings about it, protests about it and ultimately comes to some kind of resolution of the matter.

This format – conundrum, wrestling, protesting, resolution – is found in many forms of literature, from short stories to great novels as well as in poetry. Becoming familiar with such literature as deals with theological conundrums is one aspect of the study of literature within theology. But there is another side too and that is that theologians need to learn how to read literature *as literature*. The point of a story or a poem is not necessarily to entertain or to provide the reader with a pleasant (or in the case of some literature unpleasant) set of feelings, but to help them understand issues and people and history and maybe even religion and God more deeply. You won't get far in theology if you do not welcome the challenge of becoming a more sophisticated and informed reader of literature. But what's not to like about that?

There is another thing to say about literature and theology, and it involves turning the tables. English literature, in particular, is suffused with biblical imagery and language and theological references. One problem that many people have when approaching the classical texts is that they don't know enough about religion or theology to be able to understand literature. I am not advocating the full-time study of theology as something necessary if you want to appreciate Shakespeare or Dickens or Jane Austen, but there is often the prospect of a bit of a part-time job for a theologian giving literature students some of the background they need to understand their texts.

THE ANTIDOTE TO FUNDAMENTALISM

Perhaps you noticed that I have quite often used italics in this book for specific words. Theologians often do that. Rowan Williams, who was Archbishop of Canterbury from 2003 to 2013, and is one of the greatest theologians alive today, was especially fond of putting words in italics in his early writings (in fact he still does it quite a lot, though not *quite* as much). And plenty of other theologians today do the same. It's worth asking *why*.

When a theologian puts a word in italics it often means that they want you to realize that they thought quite hard before putting that particular word down, and they want you to stop and think about its particular meaning, or what it uniquely adds to the sentence.

Let me offer an example. A theologian might well write a sentence like this. 'It is important to realize that the priority for theologians is to *develop* understanding.' So 'develop' is italicized. Why might that be?

The point here is that this sentence could have read, 'It is important to realize that the priority for theologians is understanding.' But it wasn't quite that, and by adding the word 'develop' I wanted the reader to think more about what it means to 'develop understanding' than simply to understand. I can see at least three reasons for this; three reasons for stressing *develop*.

The first is to make the point that theology is not simply a matter of coming to an understanding of what others have said, though that is part of the process. It's about developing an understanding of the fundamental questions and answers that make sense in today's world.

The second is to make the point that theology is always a work in progress, is always developing because its subject matter is never going to come fully within the grasp of the human mind. Theology is not about arriving at a set of answers or a plateau of understanding but about developing a new level of understanding. Theology is the exploration of a mountain that has no summit. To engage in theology is to descend into a cave that is infinitely deep. You get the idea.

The third aspect of the word 'develop' that I hope might be picked up if the italics really did cause the reader to stop and think is that understanding might develop out of the private space of the individual thinker into a more public and communal space; the idea is that the theologian has the job of developing understanding in others, or in the community, as well as in the recesses of their own mind.

These three reasons together are why the emphasis in the sentence is on the verb 'to develop' rather than the noun 'understand'. It follows that when a theologian communicates they are not just giving a report on 'the way it is' but taking their own understanding, informed and considered as it is, into a wider arena for further consideration, reflection and, of course, *development*.

All that was a bit of a digression. If you don't like digressions you won't like theology very much, as it rarely progresses in a straightforward and linear manner. However, the digression is stopping now and we will return to the question of the importance of theology. And it is basically this. Religion is a force to be reckoned with across the world today in ways that would astonish most of the people who speculated about the future of religion and God in the nineteenth and twentieth centuries. This means that culturally we have taken our eye off the theological ball, believing that it would soon no longer be on the playing field of human civilization. The consequence is that our level of understanding of religion and spirituality is at a low ebb, and we have been caught sunbathing in the midday heat of secular modernity only to find that the tide of the sea of faith has turned and that we are now in danger of getting drenched by the rising tide of something we don't understand at all.

Let's pause for another digression. That previous paragraph was full of metaphors. Some readers might feel they were mixed; others might feel that they were artfully complex. You can decide for yourself. I don't mind. The reason to pause is to say that religious writers and theologians often use metaphors. That is, they often write or talk about something in terms of something else that is unlike it. If you like that you will enjoy theology. If you find it puzzling and want to figure it out more deeply you will enjoy philosophical theology and probably also like getting into questions of analogy. This is especially important when it comes to thinking about God because if God is different to anything else then it follows that you can't have words that are both accurate and true about God *and* about anything else. You have to talk about God using language that has developed to talk about more mundane things. In other words, if you want to talk about God in a way that people might understand you have to talk in terms of a language that should *not* be taken literally.

There are endless debates and discussions about the way in which theological language works, but you don't have to get into all that to study theology. You can if you like, however, and for some people it is pure fun, for others it is deeply fascinating and for all of us it is important that someone is thinking about these things. We are in big personal, social and cultural trouble if we accept that it's just fine to talk about God and matters of faith in a way that suggests that God is a 'thing' like other things. There is a word for this trouble and it has become an increasingly common one over the last few decades. It is *fundamentalism*.

So here's a suggestion that you might like to consider. Theology is the antidote to fundamentalism. If you agree then you may accept that it's important to study theology. If you disagree you will either be behaving like a dogmatic fundamentalist and disagreeing on principle, or you will be engaging with this as a theologian – and implicitly accepting the point that it is important to study theology – or at least to think theologically, in order to deal well with dodgy religious propositions: in this case my idea that theology is the cure of fundamentalism.

The study of theology is therefore of great importance because, unless at least some members of the human family are seriously trying to understand religion and beliefs about God and to hold constructive and critical conversations about it, then this will be the one part of life that no one understands. And you don't need to look at the newspaper headlines for long to realize that this might prove to be a very costly mistake to make. Certainly the lack of general religious knowledge and understanding among people in senior positions in local and national government, as well as in civic and commercial institutions, is already cause for concern. It would be extraordinary if in the twenty-first century we developed a good understanding of the universe and produced super-intelligent machines, discovered cures for cancer and Alzheimer's but did not have any way of knowing what different people meant when they referred to God or what was driving them when they acted on their faith.

And it may just be that there are some problems that we will not be able to solve by scientific and secular thinking. Maybe there are some completely brilliant ideas locked up inside the religions that if let free could help solve some of the major problems that face us today. For instance, there may be ideas in Islam that help us think about money in such a way as to create a more stable and just economic system. Hinduism and the religions of aboriginal and native peoples may have things to teach us that would make life more sustainable ecologically. Christianity and Judaism might teach us about how forgiveness and reconciliation in the aftermath of harmful or cruel behaviour might work in practice. And Buddhism may have the antidote to the stress of modern life in aspects of the eightfold path – indeed, the value of 'mindfulness' is an increasingly important example of this. Who would have imagined this a generation or two ago? Just about no one – which is why John Lennon's 'Imagine' has become the anthem of the generation that thought religion would die. It hasn't died. It isn't going to die. And so we ought, perhaps, to think about it with at least as much effort and energy as we think about anything else; we ought, in other words, to study theology.

If you decide to explore theology further you will need to engage in the study of religion, to find out more about history and to learn how to read works of literature as well as textbooks, essays and scripture. But you will also need to engage with some philosophical issues and for an introduction to that you can simply read on.

CHAPTER 6

PHILOSOPHY AND THEOLOGY – A PLATONIC RELATIONSHIP

There are some people who would argue that philosophy is theology's best friend. But there are several different ways of thinking about the relationship. One is that philosophy is the tool-maker and theology is the person that uses the tools. This is the sort of approach that came to its height in the twelfth century and in the writing of Thomas Aquinas. His method was very philosophical and to this day he is studied by both philosophers and theologians. There are plenty of other theologians who have used philosophical tools in an explicit way – though they do not *always* make it clear why they have used one particular set of tools rather than another.

Another way of thinking about the relationship between philosophy and theology is that theology is a more practical subject and that philosophy is dry and analytical. Theology might help you to live better or make political decisions, but philosophy will only inform you as to how logical you are being – which isn't always as much real help as very rationally minded people might think. In this relationship it is not that philosophy is supplying tools and standing in judgement over theology, deciding whether or not its arguments are good and whether its propositions make sense. This view was very strong in the period known as the Enlightenment, when some of the biggest names in philosophy wrote the books that have done so much to shape the way in which people in the Western world think and live. I am thinking of Frenchman René Descartes, who wrote that 'I think therefore I am' – finding his existence not in his body or his soul but in his thinking mind. Then there was a group of philosophers who espoused the idea that you can only really know the things that you learn though your senses. These *empiricists* set the foundations for science – though it should be noted that for many of the great scientists of this era, like Isaac Newton, science and religion were not understood to be in competition with each other. However, this strand of thinking, that philosophy can judge theology while theology has to passively accept whatever the clever clogs philosophers come up with, is not one that is very congenial to theology at all. I should be honest here and say that there were strands of philosophy in the twentieth century, such as logical positivism, an extreme form of empiricism, that convinced many people that talk about God was necessarily nonsense. This wasn't philosophy as judge but philosophy as 'god', so to speak, deciding what people may or may not talk about.

The way in which I prefer to think about the relationship between philosophy and theology, however, is as two explorers who have been travelling together for a very long time. One of them has a map, the other has a compass. One of them has a good sense of humour to keep them going when the terrain gets tough, the other has excellent eyesight to be able to see the route ahead when the rain stops and the mist lifts. One of them has a first aid kit, the other has a tent and some matches. One of them has some food, the other carries the water. You get the idea – one of complementarity. This is theology and philosophy as the yin and yang of intellectual and spiritual progress.

Thinking like this takes me back to the origins of Greek philosophy and the figure of Socrates. You won't have read a book by Socrates, because he never wrote one. In this way he was like Jesus of Nazareth. Also like Jesus he travelled around and relied on the power of conversation and words to get his ideas across. Also like Jesus he was very interested in the values by which people lived and was extremely critical of the status quo. And also like Jesus his life came to an untimely end because the authorities didn't like his teaching. And just like Jesus he was non-violent to the end and accepted his death with humility.

Socrates wasn't a monotheist, and he didn't have a positive gospel. But he did have a mission and that was to invite people to embrace uncertainty, to admit what they didn't know and to develop good character and values. As we only know Jesus and Socrates secondhand it would be wrong to claim too much for these similarities, but my own feeling is that if we only had the gospels in the New Testament and not the rather theoretical and heavy letters of Paul, then the Jesus–Socrates parallel would be more obvious and more often remarked upon.

The key point that I am trying to get across here is that there is a way of looking at both philosophy and theology as explorations. And explorations are, to my mind, journeys into the unknown. Religious people often like answers, and religious systems are often designed to provide answers and dispense certainty. This is sometimes necessary for individuals and for communities or nations and can, if done well, lead to good and worthwhile stability. But it can also become very, very dull. Neither Jesus nor Socrates was dull. They went on extraordinary intellectual journeys that took them to their deaths. This is not typical religious behaviour, which often involves obediently fitting in with the status quo and an inclination to accept hand-me-down answers rather than to ask deep questions or open up fresh perspectives. Socrates and Jesus, however, open up new paths of discipleship in which being open to wonder and letting your curiosity surface are fundamental values and practices, and where uncertainty and mystery are embraced.

This is what the best theology and the best philosophy have in common. They differ in the way they ask questions and the way they look for answers, but the difference is not complete. If theology and philosophy were expressed as Venn diagrams they would overlap – and the area of overlap is sometimes called the 'philosophy of religion'. But the overlap is greater than that because both subjects are concerned with fundamental questions of meaning and purpose and truth. And both are concerned with questions such as the following, all of which are sub-sets of philosophical theology: 'How do we know what we know?' – this is the question of *epistemology*; 'How do we read and interpret texts? – this is the question of *hermeneutics*; 'How do we know what anyone else is thinking?' – this is the area known as *theory of mind*; and 'What should we do in our lives and with our resources?' – this is the area of *ethics*. Then there is the area known as *metaphysics*. This strange word was coined by Aristotle as a chapter heading for the part of his book that came after 'Physics'; and it literally means – next to Physics. It has always been a bit of a rag bag of topics but particularly refers to questions of being and existence, as well as to questions about time and free will.

One main difference between theology and philosophy is the relevance that is accorded to Scriptures. Christian theologians, for instance, may not *defer* to what the Bible says, but they always *relate* to it in some way. Theologians also tend to take seriously what happens in spiritual and religious practices, seeing these both as ways of approaching the truth and as integral to the exploratory journey. The idea is that you will only understand some spiritual truths if you engage in certain practices or disciplines through which you seek to orient not only your mind but your whole purpose to the ultimate truth. Theologians also consider questions and issues appertaining to life before life, if I can put it that way, and life after death. Theology is concerned not only with the whole sweep of physical time but of reality beyond the constrictions of both time and space. The end of time has long been a preoccupation of religion and the theological mind, with the themes of judgement and the ultimate destiny of those who live in a new way beyond the horizon of death.

Related to this is the point that I have emphasized throughout, which is that the events that have made a deep impression on who you are will also impact on the way you see the world, interpret things, formulate questions and come to answers, conclusions and judgements. Theology is, I believe, able to be honest about this and to recognize that there is no purely objective perspective from which to make definitive judgements. Another way of putting this would be to say that theology is always a team effort. However great a theologian you are, you always need to be connecting with other people who care about the same sorts of questions but see the world differently. And however new a theologian you are – suppose this book is the first theology book you have ever read – you are invited not only to study and learn what is on the page but to think about whether it makes sense and what its implications are. Theology needs critical readers all the way along.

One way of thinking of the community of theologians – or, if you like the idea, a 'global theological team' – is to identify it with the church. This is the sort of idea that has caused some great theologians to insist that all believers are *de facto* theologians. Karl Barth, a hugely important twentieth-century Protestant theologian, thought this, and it is a strong theme in liberation theology, which has strong Catholic roots. There is even a branch of theology called 'ordinary theology' which seeks to discover and reveal what ordinary people believe before their minds get muddled and confused by church teaching. While I agree with the idea that you don't need to have a qualification to be a theologian and I definitely want to encourage many people to think theologically, I don't see the need to limit the community of theologians to the community of believers. I have already argued that an agnostic stance is actually necessary if you are to be a theologian, because theology has to be an exploration into *unknown territory*. I say this from a *theistic* perspective because I believe that God is mysterious and will never be fully known. Others can adopt a similar position as atheists, believing that there is no reality at the end of the exploration but that the journey is an interesting and important one that can illuminate our understanding of people, history and the ways in which ideas work. Not least because so many people do believe, and apparently without any reliable evidence, that there is something, though it is not a thing, that is rightly called 'God'.

There are those, as we have noted, who think that to do theology is to tell others, in no *uncertain terms*, what you believe to be the case regarding God and the ultimate questions of life. But this is not theology as exploration, or theology as quest, or theology as credible partner of science, history, literature or philosophy.

In order for theology to be credible today the individual student or teacher must be free to make up their own mind and come to their own conclusions. The *discipline* is to do this in a way that is scholarly (that is, based on a decent and critical understanding of what others have said about the matter) and that is also open to criticism and comment by others. In this way all intellectual life, theology included, but perhaps theology above all other disciplines, can be imagined as a massive, rambling conversation which can never be concluded, but in which people discover that they know more and more but at the same time realize that there is more and more that they don't know.

Theology is always in a close, almost 'spiritual', relationship with philosophy and is an exploration of the unknown that involves both personal integrity of thought and the capacity to learn from and with others as an extended team or community of people. It involves being comfortable with questions, open to new perspectives, hungry for answers but also ready to accept that even the best of answers can become the basis of new questions.

If you think you might like to travel a little with that community of explorers, then do read on.

CHAPTER 7

THE JOY OF WORDS

Although I emphasized at the beginning that theologians can and do study things like ancient works of art and contemporary films, there is no denying that if you want to study theology you have to expect to read quite a lot. More than this, you will have to wrestle with the problem that a good deal of what you are reading was written in a different language to the one you are reading it in. This is not only because there are plenty of important theologians who have not written in English; though that is true – indeed English wasn't used for theological or religious purposes in England until less than 500 years ago. Of greater significance even than this is that the religions of the three great monotheistic faiths (the faiths that believe that there is only one God), together with Hinduism and Buddhism, are based on very special books, which were written at different times and places in different languages, and go by the name of 'Scriptures'. The word literally means 'writings' and is very close to the more familiar and less loaded word 'script'.

FOUND IN TRANSLATION

The Jewish Scriptures were largely written in Hebrew. The Christian New Testament was written in Greek. The Vedas that are important for Hinduism and Buddhism were written in Sanskrit. And the Qur'an was written in Arabic. For Judaism and Christianity there is an additional complication because it is clear that Jesus, and the other characters who are reported, did not speak Greek. They spoke a local dialect of Aramaic, the language of the Hebrew people at that time. So there was a matter of interpretation even as the books were written in the first place. Paul, on the other hand, put his own thoughts on the page in Greek, so there was no prior translation going on in his letters.

Perhaps you were surprised to notice that none of these Scriptures were originally written in *Latin*. Latin was, however, a language into which the Bible was translated early on and one version, the 'Vulgate', remained the Bible that was used in the West for about a thousand years, during which time Latin was the language of the church, as it had been of the Roman Empire. For this period, which in theological terms dates from the days of Augustine to those of Luther (i.e. from about 400 to 1500 AD), most, if not all, Christian theology to the west of the Aegean Sea was written in Latin. It remains the official language of the Roman Catholic Church, but since the early 1960s members of that community have used their local language for worship, and Catholic theology has been written in huge numbers of living languages. Church law and papal decrees are still written in Latin to this day, though simultaneously issued in very many different languages.

When it comes to studying and teaching theology today, this question of language is something of a hot potato. And you will find strongly different attitudes in different institutions. There are those who think that unless you learn these languages and study the Scriptures in their original glory you can't expect to understand them, or to have anything worth saying about them. The implication of this is that any student of theology must spend a lot of time learning languages before they can get down to the intriguing questions of theology itself. There are others who think that given that a whole army of Scriptural scholars have been producing translations and commentaries for the last century or so, and as these are accessible and comprehensible to anyone who speaks English, it is now reasonable to encourage people to take a more direct route into theology.

But even that rather softer view about language learning needs to be qualified. While a theologian doesn't need to be a linguistic expert, they do need to be sensitive to some of the translation issues that exist between the Scriptural languages and their own native tongue. It is hard to see how this might be achieved without learning something about at least one Scriptural language.

But it's one thing to have a go, and another to be required to be proficient. Personally I am very much of the 'have a go' persuasion, not because I underestimate the significance of linguistic and translation issues, but because it seems to me that theology is a hugely wide-ranging subject, and that it has room for people with lots of different skill sets and areas of expertise inside its rather large tent. And also because it seems axiomatic to me that theology needs to be an inclusive team sport, as I suggested at the end of the last chapter. So, speaking personally, I feel no shame in relying on translations of texts and on commentaries, and I hope that those who work at that level are pleased that others take their work forward and use it to address issues of implication and application that they are not inclined to raise or equipped to pursue.

This is a discussion that will go on and on but it would be a pity if it were seen as one in which the serious scholars – who believe in original-language reading of texts only – were lined up against the dilettantes who believe that theological views can be appropriately formed on the basis of engaging with translations. From a Christian perspective I would want to add to the argument the point that Christianity is fundamentally *based* on translation, in that the incarnation of Jesus Christ is the expression in a new medium of the nature and reality of God. As it is put in John's gospel, 'the word became flesh'. It follows that what we primarily need to read is not the Greek words of the books we call the New Testament but the life, death and resurrection of Jesus Christ. Of course there is something to be gained from reading a text in the original language, but this would apply equally to reading various theologians, poets and novelists in their original languages. You understand differently and more deeply in the original, but you also understand when you read in translation.

It is an important Christian insight that there is no pristine, pure and entirely unequivocal version of things that you can assimilate and thereby fill yourself to the brim with theological truth. There are arguments for learning passages of Scripture by heart, but for a Christian it is not an essential activity – as it is, for instance, in Islam where the very words of the Qur'an are understood to be the words Allah dictated to Mohammed – in a quite literal sense. Put simply, Greek is not in the same relationship to Christian theology as Arabic is to Islamic theology.

Nonetheless linguistic knowledge can be both clarifying and revealing, and learning about languages and being sensitive to words is necessary if a journey of theological exploration is going to be worthwhile.

THREE WORD-STORIES

And there is another point too, which is slightly different to the translation issue. In theology words matter a lot, and a huge amount can depend on the ways in which words are used and the particular word that is chosen. Like every other subject, theology has its jargon, but in theology's case the jargon can be especially tricky as some of the words that are key to it have been on a long and complicated journey across cultures and down history before coming to us today.

Take, for instance, the word 'dogma'. This is derived from a Greek word meaning 'teaching', which also has connotations of 'standpoint'. It started life in ancient Athens, and the word 'dogmata' was used to mean 'the particular teachings that distinguish one school of thought from another'. At that time the word 'dogma' was used both to mean a teaching and a decree. But these are different things. A 'teaching' is an opinion that you can challenge and a decree is an 'edict' that you have to obey. So, what does the word 'dogma' mean in theology? Well, in Christianity the two meanings were blended together so that a 'dogma' came to mean a 'decreed teaching'; clearly this is something that not everyone will agree with but that you must accept if you want to be part of the community.

But there is another twist in the meaning of dogma too – for there is a branch of Christian theology known as 'dogmatics'. Now this is not, as you might think, the matter of learning and believing all the non-negotiable decreed teachings of the church. Nor is it the study of the kind of person who is dogmatic in their approach to theology – as opposed to being open-minded and reasonable. On the contrary, 'dogmatics' is the critical study of core theological teachings; the intelligent exploration of what is meant by the central teachings of Christianity. It follows that for a theologian, 'dogmatics' is not an exercise in dogmatism, but exactly the opposite. Having read this you can see why, but it is obvious that this is potentially very confusing.

Another, very different, word-story concerns what is arguably the most important concept in Christianity – the concept of 'love'. 'God is love' wrote John, and Paul wrote that it was the most enduring of God's gifts.[1] But what is love? Indeed, is love just one thing? As you (now) know the New Testament was written in Greek. You may be surprised to learn that Greek has four words for love. But only one of these is being referred to in the passages in John and Paul to which I have referred, and that is the word 'agape'.

Now, here comes the story of the translation of agape into English. First, the word 'agape' was translated into Latin and the word chosen was 'caritas'. Centuries later, the Latin Bible was translated into English and 'caritas' was translated as 'charity'. Back in those days charity didn't mean what it means today. It meant something like the relationship between people in a community. That's not far from the original meaning of 'agape', but it includes traces of another Greek word meaning love – 'philia'. Still, it was an acceptable translation and when people read about 'faith, hope and charity' it didn't sound odd to them – though it does to us today, which also needs to be explained.

During the Victorian era the word 'charity' was increasingly used to express practical help given to the poor and destitute, and the financial giving of 'philanthropists' (notice that the word 'philia' is in that word) needed to support it. In the twentieth century people began to feel critical of Victorian approaches to charity as they seemed not to address questions of social justice but accepted very great differences in wealth and privilege between the haves and the have-nots. Moreover, it was only the haves who could, by the exercise of philanthropy, be charitable. Yet it is clear that the capacity to love, to have or express what is called 'agape' in the New Testament, doesn't depend on wealth. So, while the translation from 'agape' to

1 See 1 John 8.4 'Whoever does not love does not know God, for God is love.' And 1 Corinthians 13.13 'And now faith, hope, and love abide, these three; and the greatest of these is love.' (NB References to the Bible are given in the standard form: Book Chapter.Verse. The two references above are from letters – in fact, most of the books in the New Testament were originally letters.)

'caritas' to 'charity' had once made sense it was now nonsense and the translators rightly decided to translate 'agape' as 'love'. The problem we are left with, however, is that while the word 'love' is today a more acceptable word in English than 'charity' it is also a very ambiguous word and doesn't distinguish between the four Greek meanings. One of those meanings is 'eros' or 'love as desire', which is not what 'agape' is about, although the passage from Paul is often read at weddings when it is erotic love that is being celebrated.

Finally in this brief section about the multiple meanings of words we come to a little family of words that describe either the content of faith or the attitude of the believer. I mean the words 'faith', 'belief' and 'creed'. These are all key words when it comes to theology, and if you were to ask most people today they would say that they all have quite a clear meaning. To believe something is to take the view that it is the case. It's a word that is used when you don't *know* but are for all intents and purposes sure enough to take a stand, or place your trust. We believe something when we have been persuaded that it is true. The word 'faith' means something similar. A person of faith is a person who adheres to a set of ideas that can't be proved. To have faith means to believe something.

As I write all this I imagine the reader nodding and thinking, 'Er, so what, this is a bit obvious.' But do bear with me.

We come now to the word 'creed' which is a noun describing a statement of belief. In order to clarify its position on matters of faith, the Church has on several occasions produced statements of core beliefs known as a 'creed', which is derived from the Latin word 'Credo'. This is the first word of such statements, and means 'I believe'. The first of these to be formulated was the Apostles' Creed, which was not written by the first followers of Jesus, although they were known as apostles, but at least one hundred if not two hundred years later. The second major creed, the Nicean Creed, was written in the fourth century and the third, the Chalcedonian Creed, was formulated in the middle of the fifth century. Clearly Christianity has been up and running as a religion, so to speak, a long time before it had sorted out its core beliefs. This might surprise many modern people, who would expect a religion first to clarify what its core beliefs are and then to apply them to life and persuade others to do the same. However, that's not the way it has worked – which raises the question of what 'belief' means.

If you step back a bit from the words that I have mentioned you find that the way in which I have described the meaning of these words is quite a *modern* way of understanding them. If you go back to the Greek, the word that ends up in modern translations as belief or faith is the word 'pistis'. And 'pistis' means, as Caroline Armstrong helpfully puts it in her book *The Case for God*, 'trust; loyalty; commitment' – which is a helpful expansion of the sometimes limited concept of 'faith', which is often understood to refer to holding the firm conviction that something improbable or unlikely really is the case.[2] The word is more to do with there being a relationship that has a certain quality. So to have faith in God is not primarily to believe in God but to relate to God, and to trust in God in a certain way. In other words, while it is difficult to imagine an atheist having faith, an agnostic might. An agnostic might be unsure that God exists, or clear that they don't know all sorts of things about God, but also live in such a way as is trusting in God and is loyal, say, to the teaching of Jesus and the life and fellowship of their local community of believers.

When it comes to the word 'belief' we can also go behind the scenes and learn that it has its origins not in holding that improbable things are true but in a Middle English word that means 'to love' or 'to prize' or 'to hold dear'.

---

2   Caroline Armstrong, *The Case for God: What Religion Really Means* (London, Vintage Books, 2010), p.350.

And when it comes to the word 'creed' the interesting thing is that it is not a word that primarily refers to what is going on in the mind or intellect, but to the heart, 'cor'. It derives from the phrase 'cor do' meaning 'I give my heart'. This, as we know, involves more than giving one's assent to a proposition.

Ultimately all these words go back to the Greek word and idea of 'pisteo', which means trust and loyalty. This is hugely significant. It suggests that 'faith' is not so much a matter of what goes on in the mind as what goes on in the heart. A matter of 'attitude' would be a more modern way of putting it. Also, faith is not something that is a property of an individual considered in isolation but is a quality of outlook that only makes sense in terms of relationship, even if that relationship is with something that is always going to be to a significant degree uncertain and unknown. Put this way you can see that *faith is not about being clear about what you know, but learning to live with what you don't know*. Or perhaps, as in the case of a relationship between ordinary people, there is an element of knowing and unknowing, history and mystery, in the relationship – and it is this mix that keeps it alive and fresh, human and worthwhile. True faith is all these things, which is why wise religious leaders all esteem it so highly. The fact that less wise religious leaders in the modern world collapse faith down to a matter of intellectual assent to things that don't seem quite right should not distract us from the sophistication and power of true faith.

Spelling all that out makes me wonder whether those people who say that you have to read Scriptures in their original languages to understand what they are really saying have got a good point. But the point doesn't stop at Scriptural languages. It extends to Latin and all the languages in which people have written theological books. That's a lot of languages, and so even if it's just for pragmatic reasons it remains my view that the important thing for someone who is God-curious is to understand the issues of theology and its most closely related subjects – philosophy, history, literature and religious studies – and to focus on becoming not a proficient linguist but a mature theologian. Although becoming a mature theologian will certainly involve understanding, in ever more nuanced ways, how language works, and dwelling on the meaning of individual words.

BOOKS AND LIBRARIES

We have already discussed the idea that theology is talking or writing or in any other way producing words about God. Inevitably the words that have been captured in books are those that have been most powerful in shaping the disciplines and practices of academic theology. And you will not find a *serious* theologian who is not in some sense interested in books. I distinguish here between a serious and a non-serious theologian because anyone can just start talking about God at any time and without thinking for two seconds about what they are saying or about how it connects with what anyone else has said or thought in the past. There is a surprising amount of this around today, as there was in the first few centuries after Christ. So much so that people such as Gregory Nazianzus, who lived in the fourth century, wrote in terms that were rather blunt about what qualified someone to discuss theology. 'It is not for all people, but only for those who have been tested and have found a sound footing in study, and, more importantly, have undergone, or at the very least are undergoing, purification of body and soul.'[3]

Whether any of the bar-room theologians took any notice is another matter, but it's important to realize, when beginning to engage with theology, that the difference between utter

---

3   Gregory Nazianzus, 'The First Theological Oration No 27: An Introductory Sermon against the Eunomians.' In *On God and Christ*, translated and introduced by Lionel Wickham (New York, St Vladimir's Seminary Press, 2002), p.27.

nonsense and deeply wise statements may not immediately be apparent to someone who is coming to the issues for the first time. You could say that we need to 'prepare' ourselves if we want to engage helpfully with theology, and note that for Gregory this preparation is a matter not only of thought but of 'body and soul'. He also asks himself who should listen to discussions of theology, and answers that it is those who take it seriously, stressing that theology is 'not just another subject like any other for entertaining small-talk, after the races, the theater, songs, food, and sex: for there are people who count chatter on theology and clever deployment of arguments as one of their amusements'.[4]

The seriousness of theology need not detract from its fascination and fun, as I have put it in an earlier chapter, but Gregory's point does suggest that it is appropriate to engage with theology with a certain amount of respect. And today one might argue that the respect can be both for the subject matter itself and for the importance that it has in other people's lives and values. Quite how seriousness is expressed and measured is not something about which our culture is currently agreed, but there is no doubt that in the recent past someone would definitely consider themselves serious as a theologian if they not only studied it carefully but also ventured into print. Not so much 'publish and be damned' as 'publish and become a theologian', one could say.

When I think of the number of books that have been written that could be described as theological – that is, are an attempt to contribute to our understanding of God, faith, religion and the 'transcendent unknown' – my mind boggles. Ask anyone who works for a removal company what it's like to move someone into or out of a vicarage. They will almost certainly groan and mention 'the books'. Those book-lined studies may increasingly

---

4   Nazianzus, 'The First Theological Oration No 27', p. 27.

be something of the past – the modern vicarage has fewer bookshelves than the grand old ones, and the modern vicar is, like the modern anything else, less book-oriented than the not-so-modern version. Things are changing, but the bookishness of theology is significant, so let's briefly explore the background to this strange phenomenon.

One of the reasons for all these books is that medieval Benedictine monasteries prided themselves on their learning and developed tremendous libraries. They were, so to speak, the universities of the pre-university era. The result is that acquiring books has been integral to the actions of those who seek to be able to speak in a wise and informed way about life's deeper questions ever since. It is increasingly hard to remember the pre-Google days, but there was a time when if you wanted to find something out you either had to ask someone or open a book. Rectories and vicarages did not have libraries on the scale of pre-Reformation monasteries, but they did have *studies* (not offices), and their occupants were expected to be both literate and learned. That is why clergy were called, and still are officially called, 'clerks in holy orders'.

This clerical bookishness is a reality but it is only part of the story of what you might call the religious book industry – and not the most important part. The more fundamental reason for all these books is that people have since time immemorial sought to talk about faith and the issues it raises, and when the scope of the late-night conversation, the occasional letter and the erudite sermon has been exhausted, they have then wanted to extend that effort and enquiry into writing, both so that they could say more, and so that more people could engage with their thoughts. And once that process begins, with a subject as open-ended and mysterious as theology, there is no stopping it. As we have already noted, the 'new atheists' are great book-writers and many shops very much like promoting their works, not to mention those of so-called New Age writers. Mind, Body, Spirit indeed! Perhaps this is how theology should re-brand itself today – the subject that connects all this speculation and spirituality with the history of religion and with philosophical and literary studies.

And it's not just books – professionally edited, printed, bound and apparently authoritative documents. If we want to study the development of human thinking about faith – to study the history of theology – we will not be able to limit ourselves to 'books' or rational arguments. Often theology develops not through cool dispassionate exchanges between wise and careful individuals who respect each other deeply, but through arguments in the sense of a full-blown row in the course of which people curse and anathematize each other. It is all in the interests of truth, of course, but when passions get roused, as they should when we realize that the stakes are very high when it comes to discerning the difference between truth and falsehood or error, even the most sincere truth-seeker can get distracted and find themselves seeking not only to identify error but to shoot down, and forever silence, the mistaken messenger.

For a student of theology, then, there is a lot to read and a great deal to engage with. There are debates to join, concepts to conjure, propositions to play with, ideas to respond to, avenues to explore; in short there are all sorts of possibilities to have fun with. No one will today read everything that has been written about theological questions, and there is no doubt that when the most well-read contemporary theologian dies there will be very many books that they had yet to read. It makes you wonder whether there is a library in heaven. After all, as someone once said, whenever God has something to say, he publishes a new book. First it was the Old Testament, then the New Testament, then the Qur'an. And so it might go on. Sikhs have their book, dating from about 1500, though the Guru Granth Sahib is treated as much more than a book, as it is regarded as the embodied spirit of God. And the Church of Jesus Christ of Latter Day Saints considers the Book of Mormon, which dates from the nineteenth century, to be God's message.

THEOLOGY AND THE MEDIA OF THE DAY

It has often been noted that, just as Christianity depended for its extraordinary expansion on the existence of the Roman Empire, so the Reformation depended for its influence and success on the invention of the printing press. It will not have passed readers of this book by that we are currently in the middle of another huge and unpredictable communication revolution. There are many well-narrated aspects to this that impact on the study of theology and also on the way in which faith is communicated – so it is of both direct and indirect relevance to us. The phenomena include the existence of the internet and the digital archiving and availability of historic images and texts, as well as social media.

You can access a huge number of historic texts online. A generation ago no one could have imagined this. Also the range of books that you can order online is extraordinarily large, and if you are prepared to buy secondhand you can get significant books for no more than the price of postage. I recall the strange feeling I had when my first book became available for one penny on Amazon. Should I be proud or broken-hearted? I decided that provided the notes with the books said 'signs of wear' I should be happy. It's the unread book that authors dread, not someone picking up a secondhand copy for next to nothing.

Then there is the whole phenomenon of digital books. It is my hope that a lot of people will read this book in that form. However, I also know that the experience of reading something on a digital reader is very different from reading a book made of paper. I understand that it's been established by psychologists that people remember less of what they read electronically, and maybe we don't read quite as carefully when we skim what's on a screen.

Then there is the surprising explosion, to me at least, of social media. Who would have thought that the Archbishop of Canterbury would be a tweeter – or the Pope? The Pope has millions of followers and huge numbers of people 'like' or 'retweet' his messages. The Archbishop is similar, though on a smaller scale. Personally, I do sometimes wonder about the process of prelatical tweeting, if I can put it that way. Do these important, wise and busy people just reach for their smartphone and peck out an observation or thought when the moment takes them? Or is there some process, involving numerous press officers and other officials, that needs to be followed before some carefully calculated formulation can be launched into cyberspace?

The truth is that we don't really know much about the origination of other people's tweets – any more than we know much about what realties and processes, personal and political, lay behind the writing of scriptures or substantial works of theology. And yet Twitter provides a curious but nonetheless real entry point to theology because it exemplifies something that theology always does – which is to insinuate itself into new media. While the printing press opened the way to the creation of voluminous libraries and the dissemination of long texts, and the spread of newspapers and magazines led to the sharing of ideas and extension of argument though short articles and essays, the digital era has allowed for a number of new phenomena, ranging from massive digital libraries to endless blogs (essays) and the pithy statements that are found privately in texts and publicly on Twitter and other microblogging sites.

Turning to my Twitter account right now provides a rather good example of the latter. It comes from @StPaulsLearning – '"Baptism is saying 'Yes' to our liberation in Christ, in a society which often sees our greatest freedom as going shopping" Timothy Radcliffe.'

I can unpack this a bit. First the context. Timothy Radcliffe is a Dominican friar who retired from his role as world superior of that religious community and has written a number of books. 'St Paul's Learning' is an institution to promote Christian learning at St Paul's Cathedral, London.

Now the contents. The tweet works at a number of levels. First it is incongruous to compare baptism with shopping. Second it is incongruous to connect baptism and freedom. It's also quite clever, because although supermarkets do give us choice – a kind of freedom – we often do not enjoy the experience of being in a supermarket and some of us, at least, feel rather anxious when we are faced with so much choice. The tweet therefore invites us to compare two things that are not usually compared, in terms in which we don't usually think about either. In this way it invites the person who reads it to think *what* the basis of true freedom might be in a new way, at the same time as encouraging them to reflect on an everyday activity, shopping, at the same time as thinking about God.

So for me this is a genuine and constructive theological tweet, giving rise to a number of questions. Is it true? Is it helpful? Is it creative? Does it open up an interesting and potentially significant set of thought processes? Might it start a conversation? If you have been following the drift of the argument in this book you will realize that it is the final two questions that are especially significant.

The very short text is not new in theology. Aphorisms and proverbs, sayings and quotes, rather than long and complex arguments, are often what people *remember*. They can have the capacity to be the very sharp arrow that pierces though our intellectual and emotional defences, and make us see something freshly and perhaps more deeply. This is a significant aspect of what theology is about because it is concerned with faith, transcendence and mystery.

So what I am going to try to do next is sketch out a history of theology in fewer than 20 tweets. By this I mean fewer than 20 very short quotations. Each one will need a bit of explanation, but if you are intrigued by this idea, then do please read on.

CHAPTER 8

A HISTORY OF CHRISTIAN THEOLOGY IN FEWER THAN 20 TWEETS

In this chapter I am offering an audacious shortcut to an overview of one particular strand of theology. It's the one I know best as I am literally at home in it. For want of a better phrase let's call it 'Western Christian theology'. My method is to offer 15 tweet-length quotes that tell the story of this tradition and at the same time suggest that it is energetically alive today. Each tweet has a little commentary that gives you a sense of where the quote in the tweet comes from and why it is significant.

Tweet 1
I am the Lord your God, who brought you out of the land of Egypt, out of the house of slavery; you shall have no other god before me.

This is the first of the Ten Commandments, which, according to the second book of the Bible, Exodus, were delivered to **Moses** when God appeared to him on a mountaintop (Exodus 20.2). These commandments were given to the Hebrew people after their liberation from Egypt and the consequent period of several decades of wandering around the desert. Many believe that the Exodus took place in 1446 BC, but quite when it was first recorded in writing is another matter. Some suggest that this happened in the sixth century BC, several hundred years after the event.

This commandment is a clear statement of the absolute importance of recognizing the uniqueness and primacy of this liberating and faithful God. The one that follows reinforces it, saying that humans must not make idols or 'likenesses'. Together they are the tap root of unequivocal and authoritative monotheism in Judaism, Christianity and Islam.

Tweet 2

You shall not take vengeance or bear a grudge against any of your people, but you shall love your neighbour as yourself.

This is one of hundreds of laws encapsulated in the book of **Leviticus**, which also dates back to the time of Moses (Leviticus 19.8). Many of them concern religious and ritual behaviour but I have included this particular one because many people think that it was Jesus who taught people to love their neighbours as themselves. Not so. The idea is deeply important, indeed integral, to Judaism.

Jesus (himself a Jew, of course) did promote this attitude, but also added something different:

> You have heard that it was said, 'You shall love your neighbour and hate your enemy.' But I say to you, Love your enemies and pray for those who persecute you, so that you may be children of your Father in heaven; for he makes his sun rise on the evil and on the good, and sends rain on the righteous and on the unrighteous. (Matthew 5.43–5)

But whether it is neighbour or enemy that is in focus, the point remains that it is a religious duty not only to relate well to God but also to other human beings.

Tweet 3

I hate, I despise your festivals, and I take no delight in your solemn assemblies… But let justice roll down like waters, and righteousness like an ever-flowing stream.

These words date from the eighth century BC and come from the lips of **Amos**, who was one of the Jewish prophets (Amos 5.24). It's often thought that prophets foretold the future, but the far greater emphasis is on telling people off because they are getting their religion wrong. Or, to put it more theologically, rebuking them because they have misunderstood what God demands of them. This is an important passage as it says that God is more interested in justice than in religious ceremonies. This, like the commandment to love your neighbour, is the root of the strand of theology known as *ethics*.

This is not an 'add-on' to theology in the Judeo-Christian tradition, but something in there from the start. The idea that religion can be disconnected from what we actually do is alien to this tradition.

Tweet 4

Jesus asked, 'but who do you say that I am?' Simon Peter answered, 'You are the Messiah, the Son of the living God.'

One of the most important questions that the New Testament books known as gospels seek to answer is the question of who Jesus is. This verse comes from the middle of **Matthew's** gospel (Matthew 16.16). Jesus and his disciples are at a Roman city called Caesarea, which is not a new settlement but a take-over of an old pagan place dedicated to the god Pan.

This is a big statement about the supreme importance of Jesus. He is the chosen or 'anointed' one, who has been sent to set God's people free. Theology today continues to explore this question of who Jesus is or was – often under the title 'Christology'.

This quote is also interesting as this is one of the very rare occasions where the apostle Peter gets something right. Mostly he gets things wrong. And yet it is Peter who becomes the leader of the disciples after the death of Jesus. This is symbolic of the profound significance of ongoing learning in the Christian tradition.

Tweet 5

Now there were devout Jews from every nation under heaven living in Jerusalem. And at this sound the crowd gathered and was bewildered, because each one heard them speaking in the native language of each.

This comes from the Acts of the Apostles, which is the second of two books of the New Testament written by **Luke** (Acts 2.5&6).

It is included here for two reasons: first, because it refers to the coming of the Holy Spirit – who is to replace Jesus on earth, and who theologians came to understand as just as much 'God' as Jesus or indeed the utterly transcendent God who appeared to Moses on the Mountain, or whom Amos declared to prefer justice to ceremony; second, because it is a clear statement that the new religion is not a religion for just one ethnic group or one language community but for people of all races and nations.

Tweet 6

We have been buried with [Christ] by baptism into death, so that, just as Christ was raised from the dead by the glory of the Father, so we too might walk in newness of life.

This is from a key passage in one of the letters of **Paul**, the letter to the Romans which was written sometime between AD 55 and 58 (Romans 6.4). Paul's letters make up a lot of the New Testament, though Luke's writings are in fact more voluminous. I have chosen it because it is an interpretation both of the resurrection of Jesus and of the rite of baptism. According to this passage, resurrection is not about life after death so much as it is about 'newness' of life. Exactly what this 'newness' is, is in my view a really important theological question, and I think that much recent theology is an attempt to answer it. It is *not* the same question as whether people have souls that might live for ever. It *is* the question of how to live in this world if we seek not only to believe in a certain religion but to be faithful to its teachings.

The passage is also important in that it refers to baptism as a step towards this newness of life, thereby suggesting a reason for baptism which is very different to what used to be taught, that we baptize people to save them from hell, or what is today most commonly taught, that we baptize people to welcome them into the church. Quite what resurrection and baptism really mean... Well, they are great theological questions because to answer them involves thinking about both theory and practice in the past and in the present.

Tweet 7
O God, you have made us for yourself and our hearts are restless until they find their rest in you.

This is our first tweet from beyond the Bible. It is from the first chapter of the first book of **Augustine's** *Confessions*.[1] Augustine lived in North Africa in the fourth century and what he saw of the demise of the Roman Empire had a significant influence

---

1   Saint Augustine, *Confessions*, translated by Henry Chadwick (Oxford, OUP, 1991).

on his outlook. Augustine started to write *Confessions* in the year 397 when he was about 40 years old. It takes the form of an extended prayer, and explores Augustine's own faith journey while delving into some deep philosophical themes.

The words of our tweet are very famous and often quoted in prayers today. It's significant that Augustine uses the word 'heart' rather than 'mind' – 'our *hearts* are restless' has a different feel to the phrase 'our *minds* are restless'. Theology is concerned with ideas and thoughts and all the things that minds do, but it's more than that. We have already seen that behaviour, what people really do, is significant. But when theologians take the word 'heart' seriously they are referring to something else. Quite what this something else is, is a matter of real importance to theology, as we explore further in the next chapter.

Augustine wrote in Latin and has had a huge influence on Western thinking in general and theology in particular. This influence may not be so great in the future as other voices become more prominent and the Western tradition looks beyond its traditional horizons to learn from other cultures and traditions, but over the last 1400 years it has been unrivalled, at least in the West.

Tweet 8
The grace of God does not replace nature, but fulfils it.

We leap forward about 850 years to get to **Thomas Aquinas**. And we move to Paris, where the Dominican friar was teaching at one of the new universities. Although he tried to teach the traditional syllabus he soon got disillusioned with it and decided to write his own new theology curriculum. So you could think of his great multi-volume work the *Summa Theologica* as a new and complete programme of theological studies.[2]

---

2 Thomas Aquinas, *Summa Theologica: A Concise Translation*, edited by Timothy McDermott (London, Methuen, 1991).

One reason Aquinas was dissatisfied with the courses on offer was that he had been studying a lot of Jewish and Islamic books as well as works of Greek philosophy – in particular Aristotle. So he wanted to work everything out from scratch, taking as little for granted as possible – assuming almost nothing. Thomas's work is written in such a way as to suggest that many of the first thoughts that people have about theological matters are wrong. This doesn't mean that they are unreasonable or absurd. It's rather that when you think about matters more deeply, and take more into account, their limits become apparent, and something closer to truth emerges from the thinking process.

His writing is especially important because he is very clear that God is not and cannot be a thing like any other thing. This quote, which comes from the very first part of the first section of the *Summa*, emphasizes that God's relationship with creation is positive and constructive. God's 'transcendence' doesn't in any way diminish or demean this world (one translation says that Grace does not 'scrap' nature) but engages with it, and, by implication, with ordinary human beings, to bring them to fulfilment, or in the Latin in which he wrote, *perfectiat*, which many have translated 'perfection'.

Tweet 9
Sin is behovely but all shall be well and all shall be well and all manner of thing shall be well.

It's not obvious from the name, but **Julian of Norwich** was a woman. In fact, she was the first woman to write a book in the English language. She lived in the fourteenth century and was an ordinary person of the merchant class.

The story behind her book is that when she was about 30 years old she became very ill. While she, and everyone else, thought she was on her deathbed she had a series of visions which she believed were 'revelations' about the nature of God.

When she recovered, she wrote down what she remembered. That was Book 1, her shorter work. Twenty years later she wrote a further book exploring their meaning even more deeply and at greater length. The two versions are often published as one book under one title, such as *Showings* or *Revelations of Divine Love* – it seems that Julian did not specify titles per se.[3] For centuries, Julian's writing was neither well known nor influential, but it was rediscovered in the first half of the twentieth century and is now being taken more and more seriously.

One of the most impressive things about Julian is her capacity to dig deeper and deeper into a subject and, as she does so, to express her different layers of wonder and question on the page. This short quote, which comes from the 27th chapter of her longer, later book, is a summary of her extensive reflection on the subject of sin. She wrestles with questions such as: 'Why are human beings sinful?', 'Why can't we seem to get over it?', 'Why does God allow us to be sinful in the first place?' She comes to the conclusion that sin is 'behovely'. This early English word doesn't have an adequate translation today, but if we think of the gap between 'necessary' and 'inevitable' we are in the right territory. And having said that sin is necessary and/or inevitable or, if you like, 'part of the process of human living', she goes on to state her profound and hard-won hope that 'all shall be well'.

It has often been assumed that Julian was a nun but recent scholarship argues against this – if she were she would probably have written in Latin.[4] The actual truth is, however, more impressive. She was an ordinary person who wrote in the same language as people lived their lives. Her approach to theology may not have been very influential in the past, but it may well be that in the future theology will be much more Julian-like.

---

3   Julian of Norwich, *Showings,* translated by Edmund Colledge and James Walsh (Mahwah, NJ, Paulist Press, 1978).

4   Veronica Mary Rolf, *Julian's Gospel: Illuminating the Life and Revelations of Julian of Norwich* (Maryknoll, Orbis Books, 2013).

Tweet 10

The proper subject of theology is man guilty of sin and condemned, and God the justifier and Savior of man the sinner.[5]

Perhaps the most significant event in the story of Western Christianity to date was the Reformation of the sixteenth century, and the most significant person in the Reformation's great cast and crew was **Martin Luther**. Like many theologians, Luther was a larger-than-life personality. He was passionate and prolific – his collected works run to over 60 large volumes. And he was hugely influential, not only on the theological stage but also on the historical stage.

Luther was a tireless thinker and a relentless opponent of those whom he thought to be wrong, such as Aristotle, the Pope and various Dominican theologians of his time. But the main thing about Luther is that he was a deeply dedicated disciple of Augustine. In fact, until he left because he thought that monasticism was a mistake, he was an Augustinian friar. But, although he left the monastery, he never left his conviction that Augustine was right about the human condition. Human beings are 'guilty of sin' and, unless saved by an outside agency, condemned to hell.

This radical negativity was, however, trumped by two astonishing realities. First, God had become a human being in Jesus Christ. Second, by dying on the cross Jesus had in some way dealt with the problem of human sin so that, although in truth we are all guilty, God does not relate to us as if we are guilty. Many theologians have spent a great deal of time on the question of *how* it is that the death of Jesus dealt with sin and reconciled God and humanity. For Luther, however, it was not so much the philosophical *how* of this as the consequences

---

5   *D. Martin Luther's Werke Kritische Gesamtausgabe*, Volume 40, II: 328. Quoted in Carter Linberg (ed.), *The Reformation Theologians* (Oxford, Blackwell, 2002), p.53.

for the way in which a Christian believer should live that were important.

For Luther, people who have faith are always sinners, and yet always 'justified', that is, treated by God as if they are not sinners. As far as he is concerned, making an effort to get on good terms with God and win your own place in heaven is a very serious mistake. First, you can never, as a sinful human being, get to the point where you can deal with the problem of your own sinfulness because that sinfulness is not just a matter of things you say and do but of something deeply wrong with you. The theological jargon for this deep and irreparable problem in human beings is 'original sin'.

And second, to try to do this would be to try to do something that God has already done; which is foolish, discourteous and ultimately blasphemous.

Luther is serious about sin but even more serious about *grace*. The word 'grace' refers to the generosity of God that heals and restores damaged human beings. It is this grace that deals with sin and it does so without effort or *work* on the part of the sinner. The task of the sinner, therefore, is not to sort themselves out, except in the sense of learning to believe in, accept and respond to the grace of God which was revealed and liberated once and for all in the cross of Jesus Christ.

It follows that for Luther the cross is supremely important, which is why he wrote that the task of a theologian is to be a person who 'comprehends the visible and manifest things of God seen through suffering and the cross'.[6]

Tweet 11
You must sit down, says Love and taste my meat:
so I did sit and eat.

---

6   From 'The Heidelberg Disputation', April 1518. Quoted in E.G. Rupp and Benjamin Drewery (eds), *Martin Luther* (London, Edward Arnold, 1970), p.21.

These words come from a poem by **George Herbert** called called *Love (III)* in which God is seen as offering an eternal banquet to which the human person is invited. Yet the invitee feels unable to accept because they are a sinful mortal. As the poem unfolds it is made clear that God understands all this, but nonetheless insists that the mortal sinner is more than welcome.

Herbert was born in 1593 and as a young man became a high-ranking member of the University of Cambridge. He was later ordained and was a parish priest for the final three years of his short life. During this time he wrote a book to advise other clergy regarding their duties, and how to discharge them, called *A Priest to the Temple*. He also wrote poems and when he, rightly, felt he was dying sent them to Nicholas Farrar of Little Gidding who had them published by Cambridge University Press in September 1633, Herbert having died in March.

The poems have been hugely influential on the way in which English-speaking people have understood their faith and spirituality. They are often seen alongside the poetry and sermons of his seventeenth-century contemporaries John Donne, who was a family friend, and other metaphysical poets like Henry Vaughan. These poets all have a sense of the deep mystery of God and they recognize that the human quest to understand and respond to God's love is strangely difficult. Vaughan wrote that, 'There is in God, some say, / A deep yet dazzling darkness.'[7] And Donne, surprisingly, invited God to 'Batter my heart.'[8]

I have been referring here to 'God' but Herbert does not refer to God in the poem but to 'Love'. It begins with these words: 'Love bade me welcome, yet my soul drew back, guilty of dust and sin...' The point being made throughout the poem is that

---

7   Henry Vaughan, 'Night'.
8   John Donne, *Holy Sonnets*:
     'Batter my heart, three-person'd God, for you
     As yet but knock, breathe, shine, and seek to mend;'

God really is Love and can be related to as one who loves, and understood through our own experience of loving and being loved.

The imagery of being nourished, and the Christian sacrament of Holy Communion where bread and wine are blessed and shared as the body and blood of Christ, is very strong. Modern churchgoers may be surprised by the picture painted in the last line of *sitting* to eat and drink the nurturing gifts of God. In fact, Herbert himself was in two minds about it, as his biographer, John Drury, points out by quoting Herbert, who wrote that, 'The feast indeed requires sitting, because it is a feast; but man's unpreparedness requires kneeling.'[9]

Tweet 12
From the age of fifteen, dogma has been the fundamental principle of my religion...religion, as a mere sentiment, is to me a dream and a mockery.

Like Herbert, **John Henry Newman**, from whose autobiography this quote is taken, was an Anglican priest.[10] However, unlike Herbert, he moved out of the Church of England, becoming a Roman Catholic and ultimately a cardinal. Born in 1801, he lived through most of the nineteenth century, and was one of the leaders of the Oxford Movement before converting to Catholicism. The Oxford Movement stressed the continuity of the Church of England with the pre-Reformation Catholic Church and the importance of the symbolic and dramatic aspects of religious practice, especially encouraging the use of sacraments – that is, symbols and practices that help people

9   John Drury, *Music at Midnight: The Life and Poetry of George Herbert* (London, Penguin, 2014), p.3.
10 John Henry Newman, *Apologia Pro Vita Sua* (London, Fontana, 1959), p.132 (first published 1884).

appreciate and accept the grace of God as a gift to sustain and bless their lives in this world.

What this little quotation clarifies is that for Newman religion is not about emotion, or, as he puts it, 'mere sentiment'. He uses the word 'dogma' which we discussed earlier, and in this case suggests propositions that have intellectual rigour and clarity. It is very interesting that he says that this has been the case for him since he was 15 years old. Teenage years are often understood to be emotional times, but perhaps it is also a time when the religious quest is one in which the desire for intellectual clarity has, for some at least, a special importance.

Tweet 13

Take your Bible and take your newspaper, and read both. But interpret newspapers from your Bible.

If Newman was reacting against the overly emotional nature of some of the religious influences that were important in the very early nineteenth century, **Karl Barth** came to react even more intensely to the intellectual liberalism of the middle and later years of the same century. Barth lived from 1886 to 1968. The First World War had a huge impact on the way in which he understood life and sought to find meaning and purpose, as it did on many of his generation. His first main publication came out in 1919 and was a commentary on Paul's letter to the Romans. It a trenchant and direct book and many have called it *prophetic.*

While nineteenth-century liberals were content with an optimistic view of human nature and were positive about the capacity of human beings to get on well with each other and with God and make *progress*, Barth read the Bible with eyes made sensitive by unimaginable suffering. The result was that Barth felt the need to emphasize the themes of the complete *otherness* of God, the sinfulness of humanity and the need for all this to be reconciled afresh in a direct and trenchant way. There was no use, for Barth, in pretending that it was easy to put things right or that God could really be understood or apprehended by the likes of us. Theology could only proceed if God shaped and controlled our thinking: something that God had, in fact, taken in hand by becoming human in Jesus Christ. It is the person, life, death and resurrection of Jesus Christ that, according to Barth, reveal God's true and full nature. In short, according to Karl Barth, if you want to know what God is like, you should consider Jesus Christ.

Second, and as part of this, Barth developed the overarching idea of the supreme significance of the *word* of God – the means whereby humans can come to some sense of divine knowledge. Barth is therefore a theologian who takes the Bible extremely seriously. And yet for Barth there is no cosy little religious world where isolated individuals can curl up with their Bibles or where detached groups can sit around having prayer meetings oblivious to politics and current affairs. And this is the point of the quotation that I have used as a tweet which actually comes from an interview in *Time* magazine and concerns advice that the theologian remembers giving to young theologians in the 1920s.[11] The Bible must always be at hand but so too must the newspaper. He doesn't mean this literally, of course. The Bible here represents the word of God and the newspaper the life, concerns and crises of our fellow human beings. These things must be connected, declares Karl Barth. And he is adamant. It is the Bible that must interpret the newspaper, not vice versa.

Like Augustine, Aquinas and Luther, Barth was an extremely prolific writer and his greatest project, a 14-volume spiralling and encyclopaedic work running to 8,000 pages in the English translation (it's longer in German), is called *Church Dogmatics*.[12]

11   'Barth in Retirement', *Time*, 31 May 1963.
12   Karl Barth, *Church Dogmatics*, edited by G.W. Bromiley and T.F. Torrence (Edinburgh, T. & T. Clark, 1957).

Tweet 14

There are not two histories, one profane and one sacred, 'juxtaposed' or 'closely linked.' Rather there is only one human destiny.

While nineteenth-century liberal theology was seen to be too soft and pliable to have anything to say to people in the aftermath of war, twentieth-century liberation theology has often been seen to be so harsh, unaccommodating and divisive as not to have anything to say to anyone enjoying a pleasant standard of living or good health. Liberation theology was born in Latin America and the Peruvian **Gustavo Gutierrez**, who is quoted here, was one of its pioneering architects; his book, *A Theology of Liberation*, from which this tweet comes, is a classic and seminal text.[13] While the true home of liberation theology is south of the equator I consider it to be part of the Western Christian tradition because most, if not all, of the theologians who were behind it were educated at universities and seminaries of Europe or North America. These theologians, often from a Roman Catholic background, became increasingly distressed by both the top-down nature of theological teaching and church organization and by the increasing economic disparity between the rich and the poor. Liberation theology in the twentieth century was informed by left-wing, socialist thinking and Marxist ideas, and all this, when mixed with a straightforward reading of the gospels, made it clear that God wasn't neutral when it came to a consideration between the huge gulf of the rich and the poor. God, as the liberation theologians put it, has a 'bias to the poor'.

The impact of liberationist perspectives might have been far greater had twentieth-century politics unfolded differently. However, the end of the century saw one of the longest papacies

---

13   Gustavo Gutierrez, *A Theology of Liberation: History, Politics and Salvation*, translated and edited by Sister Caridas Inda and John Eagleson (London, SCM Press Ltd, 1974), p.153.

in history and the Polish pope, John Paul II, had, as a parish priest, bishop and archbishop, been formed *not* by the plight of the poor in South America but by the struggle with communism behind the Iron Curtain. This meant that those Catholic theologians who embraced socialist or Marxist thinking were given an extremely hard time, and liberation theology, while not entirely silenced, was definitely put down.

Nonetheless, various forms of liberation theology remain important to this day, not least those that have moved away from a focus on 'the poor' to a focus on particular and specific groups. This is a strand that connects back to the prophetic words of Amos and the ethics of justice and which emphasizes that there really is no place or position that is neutral or from which someone can do purely objective theology – that is, develop a pure and disinterested understanding of God.

Tweet 15

Woven into our lives is the very fire from the stars and the genes from the sea creatures, and everyone, utterly everyone, is kin in the radiant tapestry of being.

Our final quote comes from a lecture that contemporary feminist theologian **Elizabeth A. Johnson** gave in 1993.[14] Feminist theology can be seen as a branch of liberation theology but has moved away from a Marxist analysis of society or a focus on specifically economic disparity. Interestingly and creatively it has expanded its range of concern to include the natural world in its broadest and most historic sense.

In *Women, Earth and Creator Spirit*, Johnson set out some themes that she subsequently developed in more recent books

---

14 Elizabeth A. Johnson, *Women, Earth and Creator Spirit* (New York, Paulist Press, 1993), p.39.

such as *Quest for the Living God* and *Ask the Beasts*.[15] She sees patriarchy and dualistic and mechanistic thinking as major problems for the Western theological tradition as they create distance and distort relationships. She also believes that the 'Creator Spirit' has not been given the same prominence as the 'Father' or the 'Son' in theology. To address these distortions she proposes three moves. The first is to listen to the voice of women who, for historical rather than intrinsic reasons, speak for 'connectedness' and a relational approach to life. The second is to attend more closely to the 'Creator Spirit' and let it have a larger influence on theological understanding. The third is to develop a 'kinship' relationship with the non-human world, rather than one of either 'kingship' or 'stewardship'.

I have noted throughout this book that theology often develops in a context of dispute and disagreement, with opponents sometimes becoming vociferous in their criticisms of each other. Elizabeth Johnson hasn't escaped this any more than her predecessors. Although her book *Quest for the Living God* received great praise when it was published it came under attack from the Catholic bishops in the United States in 2011 in a statement which described many of its conclusions as 'unacceptable'. Theologians always run the risk of reaching unacceptable conclusions when they engage properly in their work of asking eternal questions. Johnson emphasizes the unknowability of God, the importance of appreciating that theological language is metaphorical, and the theological significance of non-Christian religions and the sacredness of the whole of creation. The American Catholic bishops clearly did not like the drift of this, and felt it necessary to point out how it diverges from the teaching of the church. If theology is a quest however, as the title of Johnson's book suggests, it is inevitable

---

15 Elizabeth A. Johnson, *Quest for the Living God: Mapping Frontiers in the Theology of God* (London Continuum, 2007), *Ask the Beasts: Darwin and the Love of God* (London, Bloomsbury, 2014).

that those who engage in it are going to depart from that which is already established. However, from Johnson's point of view the point is actually more theological than the logical one that I am making. Her quest is after all for the *living* God. Not all readers of this book will feel that this is a sensible starting point for a quest, but all may agree that for a believer the prospect of relating to a living God is rather more attractive, and exciting, than relating to any other sort of God. And a living God is never going to be adequately reflected in inherited theology. Theology itself needs to live. That's what makes it fascinating, fun and important.

This brief passage that I have used as my final 'tweet' has often been quoted alongside the sentence that follows, 'This relationship is not external or extrinsic to our identity but wells up as the defining truth from our deepest being.' The idea that relationships are primary and are 'the defining truth of our deepest being' is characteristic of the kind of theology that is now emerging from the tradition that I have been describing. It is open to a response of wonder at creation (wonder which, incidentally, Johnson expects to be enhanced and not diminished by science) and is expressed in rich and almost poetic language – 'the radiant tapestry of being', for example.

Elizabeth Johnson is deeply concerned about truth. However, her sense of truth is not an idea or a set of words, or something that can be defined in a limited way, but something that 'wells up'. In writing in this way she is certainly appealing to the mind, but also to the heart, and there can be no doubt that she wants theological thinking to impact on personal and political behaviour.

REFLECTION

To suggest that the history of even one strand of Christian theology might be summarized in just 15 short quotations is to propose something quite absurd. Nevertheless, putting this list together has been an interesting exercise – at least for the writer! As I review it again it seems to me that it would be possible to make an even more condensed summary by boiling down the 'message' of each tweet to a few words. To continue the metaphor I am going to call this a history of theology in 15 hashtags, each one of which takes a key point from one of the tweets.

1   #GodisGod

2   #Loveyourneighbour

3   #Justicematters

4   #JesusisMessiah

5   #GodsSpiritisforall

6   #Resurrectionmeansnewness

7   #RestonlyinGod

8   #Graceperfectsnature

9   #Allshallbewell

10 #Gracerules

11 #Godfeedsus

12 #Truthmatters

13 #ReadtheBible

14 #Onlyonehistory

15 #Everyoneiskin

Behind these hashtags lie not only millions of words but many more thoughts and experiences and encounters, all of which have begun with some kind of open-minded reflection and questioning. It is by pursuing questions that are both immediate and potentially eternal that humanity has come, in different ways, to be able to be appropriately articulate about matters we cannot know about in the same way that we know about many other things. This disjunction in knowing has become quite awkward since the rise of science, technology and modern medicine, and this awkwardness has provoked a split between those who are happy with a materialist view of the world, and those who opt for a form of religion based not on the sort of questioning I have been espousing here, but on some kind of revealed knowledge to which believers are given special access. It is this second mindset that has made fundamentalism and literalism such a strident and certain voice today. Yet what I have shown here is that genuine theology is a careful and shared engagement with eternal questions. This is what has generated the 15 tweets, and this is what has enabled me to take this further and produce the hashtags. Indeed, it has allowed you to read them and start to think about what they mean and to consider whether they help with the questions that bubble up in your mind.

Ultimately the invitation to engage with eternal questions is the invitation to take part in a conversation that has very deep roots and a very long history, one strand of which has been summarized, inevitably very inadequately, in this chapter. It is a quest that will always seek to travel beyond the apparent horizon. So, for instance, the list of hashtags is presented both as very pithy summary and also in the hope that it might, by both its strengths and weaknesses, provoke more thoughts and questions – more conversation. For integrity's sake, this conversing and questing needs to take place in a way that is as committed, responsible, informed and creative as is possible for any particular person at any stage in life. It will also, and inevitably, take into account the preoccupations, anxieties and hopes of the era and culture in which they live.

We have seen hints of this in our survey which, in its biblical phase, starts with the basics of monotheism, flags up justice, establishes who Jesus is and what resurrection means, and adds to that the universal relevance of the Spirit. In its post-biblical phase we see a theological agenda shaped by deep concern about how a self-aware, self-anxious and bodily human being might relate to the transcendence and love of God. These issues dominate the agenda for over a millennium in which questions of sin and how it is dealt with are predominant, and yet in the late nineteenth and early twentieth century we see a strong emphasis on the possibility that theology might give voice in society to a different truth, whether this is 'doctrine' or a product of interpreting the newspaper through the Bible. Theology in this phase of Western history is becoming a bit less anguished and rather more oppositional and challenging; it is developing what one might today call 'attitude', which is not surprising given the advance of secularism and atheism and the reduced power and authority of the church. In the face of this it is understandable that the church is a bit uppity. But at its best this new-style theology is not strident or defensive, but engaged at an even more serious and significant level. It is less concerned about the happiness or ease (whether in this world or the next) of any individuals, or with the precise formulation of any proposition needed to make it timelessly truthful. Its concern is with the way in which human history, and indeed the whole ecosystem of the planet, is interrelated and bound in a common destiny where people matter hugely, yet where love is understood to mean so much more than romance or loyalty to blood relations. This might look and seem new but it is a familiar pattern. We can see it in our very first tweets where love of God and love of neighbour are quickly connected and from whence the imperative for justice emerges.

In today's world the conversation that emerges from our ordinary yet eternal questions must take into account both what we know historically and what we experience in our daily lives. But the perennial issues of personal suffering, the inability of human beings to be as good as they should be or would like to be, the scandal of manifest inequality and injustice, the impossibility of ever fully knowing some important matters with complete certainty, and sometimes great fear about the future, are always going to have a strong influence on the way in which our theological conversation flows. The vital thing is that these matters all drive the conversation forward, and that none of them are allowed to stop it in its tracks.

Theology today must be globally aware; the 24-hour news cycle and the ubiquity and speed of video accounts of what is going on in faraway places replace, in a way, the newspaper at the breakfast table and have a different kind of intellectual and emotional and spiritual impact. Theological questioning today also needs to be aware of other religions, theologies and spiritual traditions, not considering them as exotic phenomena or practices to be dismissed as alien or judged as erroneous, heretical or worthy of an 'anathema', but to be seen as different ways of pursuing the quest for truth, meaning and purpose up to and beyond the horizon of the knowable.

Theology today has a huge and complex agenda, which can perhaps be boiled down to one very short, eternal question. What really matters? Or, #whatreallymatters.

As we have seen, theology involves being both conversational and careful with words. But might it also mean going *beyond* words? If that question intrigues you, do read on.

CHAPTER 9

PICTURES, POETRY
AND GOD

Ever since the time of Moses and the Ten Commandments, written words have had an especially privileged role in communicating about God and discussing matters of faith. Theology, taken literally, means 'God-words', and, as we have seen, religious people in general, and theologians in particular, have generated them with great energy over the years.

Words are not the only ways of communicating, thinking or exploring. Human beings have made pictures for longer than they have written words down and created laws or literature. The Ten Commandments prohibited the making and worshipping of idols, which one might think of as sculptures of gods, and also the making of any kind of 'likeness' (Exodus 20.4–5). This was a problem for any would-be artists among the ancient Hebrew people and, while Jesus did turn many aspects of 'the law' upside down he is not on record as saying, 'It's okay, you can draw drawings and paint pictures of whatever you like now.'

Nonetheless after a few centuries the early Christians become quite comfortable with images and began to incorporate them into their places of worship; by the sixth century there were plenty of paintings and mosaics in churches. A distinction had been made between the making of *idols* or idolatrous images, and the creation of *icons*. Although there was resistance to this from time to time, in particular when Christianity was influenced by Islam in the eighth century and by the Protestant Reformation in the sixteenth century, images were always rehabilitated. The idea that there might be positive, appropriate and beautiful Christian art incorporating representations or likenesses developed in Protestant as well as Catholic Christianity.

Meanwhile in the regions further to the east, where Christianity was 'Orthodox' rather than Catholic or Protestant, it was a more astringent form of visual expression, 'icons' in the strict sense, that was to become accepted and normal. Unlike the pictures of Western art, icons are not understood as expressions of any artistic sentiment but are carefully 'written' within a disciplined framework involving, perhaps, constant prayer, and, in some cases, fasting. The finished works are then neither decorational nor educational but are understood as windows into the transcendent, as actually mediating the presence of the saint represented or, if the icon is of Christ, then of God. The worshipper, by looking at them, looks *through* them to the realm of uncreated light.[1]

Today, a visit to a gallery or museum will richly reward anyone seeking to understand how people in the past interpreted matters of faith through the media of shape and colour, texture and form. Some of this was understood as educational and some as a way of adding lustre and beauty to worship. However, theologians are increasingly alert to the possibility that the visual arts might provide a means not only of expressing but developing or challenging existing theological ideas or views.

---

1   A succinct and accessible introduction to the theology of icons is found in Rowan Williams, *The Dwelling of the Light: Praying with the Icons of Christ* (Norwich, Canterbury Press, 2003).

In 2002 the National Gallery in London hosted an exhibition called 'Seeing Salvation' when an array of religious artefacts was presented together with a commentary and explanation which not only gave art-historical but theological help to the visitor. There was a parallel television series, and the impact of the whole thing was widely felt, with the Gallery's director receiving an unusually large correspondence concerning the impact that the exhibition had had on those who experienced it. The theologian George Pattison was not, however, convinced that the way in which 'Seeing Salvation' presented Christian art was conducive to the kind of response that I am suggesting here. In fact he saw the presentation of religious material in a secular context, be it an art gallery or the broadcast of a papal blessing, as reduced to the level of 'event' because it had entered 'the irresistible gravitational field of the global culture industry'.[2] Pattison went on to qualify this judgement (he himself calls it harsh), and suggested the more nuanced conclusion that such art can nevertheless retain 'a vestige of an "ecclesiastical" function'.[3] I would want to develop this to suggest that art can serve an *exploratory theological purpose* when the pressure is taken off it to give visual expression to a dogma that is understood first in verbal form, or to provide an *aide memoire* for a story that has been heard and learnt orally (to be a visual aid), or to be 'functional' in any ordinary sense of the word.

What was remarkable for me about 'Seeing Salvation' was the impact of the relatively spare and cool verbal commentary on the spiritual apprehension of the objects of religious art, and the theological stimulation and inspiration that this created. While Pattison feared that Neil MacGregor's introductory essay in the catalogue moved the interpretation *away* from an 'exclusively

2   All quotes from Pattison here are from George Pattison, *Crucifixions and Resurrections of the Image: Christian Reflections on Art and Modernity* (London, SCM Press, 2009), p.16.
3   Pattison, *Crucifixions and Resurrections of the Image*, p.20.

Christian' reading of the paintings and objects, it seemed to me that his words gave permission and encouragement to the viewer to connect with what would otherwise have been an alien image precisely because it belonged in a religious context – whether that context is actual and physical (a church building, say) or the narrative context of biblical story or a clear framework of doctrine. These words from MacGregor's introduction are pivotal: 'In the hands of the great artists, the different moments and aspects of Christ's life become archetypes of all human experience… These are pictures that explore truths not just for Christians but for everybody.'[4]

Taken out of context and reported here, or in Pattison's book, they can come across as words that generalize, de-particularize and water down. However, when taken in close proximity to the actual pictures and images themselves, where the religious identities are apparent, the words could, and in my experience did, work the other way.

And not only in my experience; the sociologist of religion Grace Davie analysed all the letters that were sent to the Director in response to the exhibition and television programmes.[5] Davie notes the same point as Pattison concerning MacGregor's generalizing interpretation, but, like several critics who wrote newspaper articles about the exhibition, viewed it positively. One commentator, for instance, wrote that, 'Whatever the intentions of the Jerusalem Trust, the exhibition leaves it an open question whether these works triumph because of the subject matter or in spite of its restriction…but you don't have to believe to see that there are miracles of some kind here'. Davie emphatically

---

4   Neil MacGregor, 'Introduction.' In Gabriele Finaldi, *The Image of Christ: The Catalogue of the Exhibition 'Seeing Salvation'* (London, National Gallery Co. Ltd, 2000), p.7.

5   Grace Davie, 'The Use of Text as Data in the Sociology of Religion.' In Paul Avis (ed.), *Public Faith? The State of Religious Belief and Practice in Britain* (London, SPCK, 2003), pp.28–44.

agrees: 'This is undoubtedly so.' But quite what these 'miracles of some kind' are is perhaps the theological point at issue, and it seems to me that MacGregor has served a theological purpose not by offering answers but by juxtaposing image and word in such a way as to stimulate a process of thinking that is properly thought of as theological, whatever conclusions it may arrive at. It is precisely by taking religious images out of context, but also explaining the context, that they are able to do their work. This is not 'enchantment' but 'estrangement'. And it is, I would argue, the key that can start the theological motor.

This is perhaps one reason why the study of different religions, encounters between adherents of different faiths or visits to new cultures can be so stimulating. Theological thought is often provoked not by voluntary activities, however, but by chance encounters or eventualities or circumstances that cause us to feel shock, disappointment, anger or some other form of discomfort. The point about art is that it can give us visual and imaginative experiences that require us to engage our minds, rearrange our intellectual furniture and maybe do some decluttering or restocking. Such are, metaphorically speaking, the activities of theology when the questions in hand are deep, the implications profound and the possibilities transcendent.

Turning to the Director's mailbag, Davie found plenty of evidence that people experienced the exhibition religiously. To take just one example from someone who was not able to visit the exhibition in person but was given the catalogue by a friend, 'that alone has had a profound effect on me. The whole concept, the headings, the understanding, the insights and the sheer inspiration within the catalogue have enriched my life and my understanding of God and His purposes of us, more than I can say.'

Visual images connect and communicate in a different way to words, and reflecting on this now, I want to suggest that they do so in a way that is closer to a religious or spiritual way of thinking than words often manage. This, I suggest, is why images, idols and icons have been regarded with suspicion by religious authorities – not because of their weaknesses, but because of their *strengths* as purveyors of theology.

If this is so, we should perhaps ask *why*. Words have a lot going for them as tools of communication. We are constantly using them as we speak and as a written culture develops so too do our skills of definition. Our linguistic tools become sharp, analytical, precise and forensic. Theologians have sought to exploit these qualities of languages to allow them to develop their positons and arguments. And yet there are reasons to question whether this is, in fact, the only way for theology to develop. Might it be that the best way to understand God and faith and meaning and purpose is not by defining our terms and using them precisely but by engaging more holistically with them? After all, when we seriously try to understand another person, either when we first fall in love with them, or over the long haul of a more or less intimate relationship, we so often find that words fail us. Yet might it be that words can come to function for us not so much as tools but as icons, as Orthodox Christianity has come to understand them? Not as little packets of precise meaning, but as windows into transcendence; as ways of apprehending not a world of facts and functions but of people and relationships; as bridges not into the world of black and white, right and wrong, yes or no, but the world of shade and colour, nuance and ambiguity. And yet, as this moves us away from a model of thinking that might be mimicked by a machine based on binary code, so it moves us towards a way of knowing that is appropriate when we are thinking theologically – that is, in terms of a God who is not an object, item or thing, nor indeed a 'person' in the same way that you and I are persons.

SCIENCE AND WISDOM –
TWO WAYS OF KNOWING

A couple of very different writers offer similar suggestions as to why we might be wise to construe the theological quest as *more* than an exercise with words. The first is our old friend Augustine who, as the contemporary American theologian Mark McIntosh explains, distinguished (as did most of his contemporaries) between two forms of knowing – *scientia* and *sapienta*, 'science' and 'wisdom'.

Science is the way in which the mind relates to what it thinks it can 'grasp and master', whereas wisdom is 'a kind of knowing in which the mind is, as it were, befriended by the great truth beyond its grasp, a truth so fulfilling that its contemplation is the very consummation of human existence'.[6] According to Augustine, we human beings lost some of our better capacities at the 'fall', and this is evident in the way we think. McIntosh puts it like this: 'its fallen approach to perception and understanding now disdains contemplative wisdom and insists on utter absorption with the little self-gratifying items it can possess and manage for itself'. This is a form of knowing which is, in the end, unsatisfying. McIntosh, not intending to belittle or send up the theological enterprise, does here actually present a vivid description of what I would suggest is theology in a far too typical yet nonetheless adulterated form, interested in bits and pieces of detail but never able to behold the big picture. This is the slide into a form of knowing that is not so much wrong as inadequate. McIntosh again: 'So humanity descends into ever more anxious forms of knowledge about less and less fulfilling objects; and the more obsessively it attends to these,

---

6   All the quotes here from McIntosh are from Mark McIntosh, *Divine Teaching: An Introduction to Christian Theology* (Oxford, Blackwell, 2008), p.156.

in its small minded sort of way, the less it is any longer able to sense the divine presence.'

The second thinker to draw attention to this increasingly granular and gasping, avaricious and anxious sort of knowing is the neuroscientist Iain McGilchrist, who associates it with the functioning of the left hemisphere and a necessary but secondary role he feels it should play in the overall task of human knowing. McGilchrist sees right-hemisphere functioning as primary, and interestingly suggests that while the left brain has a great facility with words and numbers it is the right brain that we use when we encounter both human beings and works of art.[7] If we return to MacGregor's introduction to the 'Seeing Salvation' catalogue we find that he makes a similar point: 'Theological concepts must be given human dimensions and if only words can tackle abstract mysteries, paintings are uniquely able to address the universal questions through the intelligence of the heart.'[8]

We have been encouraged by Augustine, McIntosh, McGilchrist and MacGregor to open the door to seeing the non-verbal forms of thought and communication as being legitimate, if not actually *primary*, aspects of the theological quest. They all invite us to use the 'intelligence of the heart' in this project. If they are right, it would mean that, far from theology being an image-free zone, it might be that theology books ought to be illustrated, not in terms of diagrams that conveniently present condensed information, but with those forms of representation or pattern that excite our right hemisphere, connect with our heart's intelligence, and draw from us a holistic or contemplative response, which, while non-grasping and non-anxious, is nonetheless comprehending and curious.

This sort of stance is appropriate in theology, I would argue, whether it is occasioned by the variety and depth of the subject

---

7   Ian McGilchrist, *The Master and His Emissary: The Divided Brain and the Making of the Western World* (London, Yale University Press, 2009).

8   MacGregor, 'Introduction', p.7.

matter, or by respect for the adherents of different religious views or, as Augustine and McIntosh argue, by an awestruck wonder-filled contemplation of God. I would further suggest that it can be occasioned not only by visual representations, but also by other steps away from the controlling and analytical use of language, such as poetry.

THEOLOGY AS POETRY

As I reflect on the quotations used in the tweets chapter it occurs to me that to have compiled that list by focusing only on clear propositions, or without referring to poetry at least once, would have been to do a disservice to theology. Careful essays and long and carefully footnoted works of systematic theology have their place. There is no reason for human beings not to stretch their forensic intellectual faculties to the full in exercising their God-curiosity but, no matter how thorough the intellectual effort, the chances are that the account will remain in some way incomplete, and there will yet be room not only for another set of questions to be raised, but also another set of pictures to be painted or poems written.

I would like to suggest that poetry is an indispensable tool in theology, and that there is a strong case for considering it to be theology's *lingua franca*. Writing recently, Mark Oakley has perceptively contrasted a poetic approach to theology with the 'simple answers' approach. He sees poetry as intrinsically connected with theological exploration and the inexhaustibly mysterious and generous nature of its subject matter:

> The 'simple answers' approach to faith fails to recognize…
> that from its very beginnings the human intuition that the
> world is a gift, that it has a divine origin and that life and
> love come from this same source, was explored and shared

poetically. No other language could begin to do justice to these inspiriting, daunting mysteries of reality itself.[9]

Oakley observes that the Scriptures of many of the world's religions are poetic, pointing to Hinduism, Daoism, Judaism, Christianity and Islam. And he both anticipates and summarizes our argument here very precisely when he writes that, 'It [poetry] is not just a better way of saying truth but rather truth is found in that [poetic] form.'[10]

If you were to try to imagine the Christian theological tradition with all the poetry scraped out of it you would find yourself with something very, very different to theology as the questioning, exploratory, open to uncertainty and mystery quest that I have presented in these pages. Try putting doctrine, ritual and ethics together without the glue of the poetic and you would have something not only unconvincing, but also bizarre and soul-less.

Something similar could be said about music. Imagine Christianity without song, without rhythm, melody and harmony and without those inexpressible forms of fellowship, community and solidarity generated when people make or attend to music together, and you have an utterly different animal. The psalms, hymns and spiritual songs which we both encounter and read about in the Bible, and which have sustained and supported worship and contemplation ever since are not optional extras but vital to the tasks of holding, formulating, answering and moving forward with eternal questions. Let it be understood that such spiritual songs include carols, choir anthems, choruses and children's actions songs, as well as spirituals and protest songs. These are not part of the religious packages because they are moments of diversion or light relief. They are vital aspects of the human response, both questioning

9   Mark Oakley, *The Splash of Words: Believing in Poetry* (Norwich, Canterbury Press, 2016), p.xviii.
10   Oakley, *The Splash of Words*, p.xxi.

and contemplative, to whatever it is that is beyond the horizon of the obvious and the material world.

When I was working on a book on the subject of forgiveness I was very surprised to come to the conclusion that under very difficult and challenging circumstances forgiveness is an act of *creativity* that is rather like the act of writing a poem.[11] It made me wonder whether the writing and reading of poetry was in fact the highest of intellectual and spiritual activities. To make that claim would be to make a controversial value judgement – some might want to argue that it is mathematics that should take such pride of place. But let me make the smaller claim that not only are words of vital importance to the exploratory task of theology, but it is the poetic aspect of words that is just as important as their literal and precise meaning, and that it is through art and the poetics of language that theology can begin to open out and embrace its subject matter.

We could summarize that subject matter as God, love, the origins and endings of all things and all the issues that arise when human beings base their lives not on known facts but on trusted beliefs. The point being made here is that this vast area of human concern cannot be adequately addressed unless the poetic dimension of language, and the imaginative possibilities of intelligence, are deployed with the same energy and commitment as our analytical qualities of mind and our capacity for precision and distinction.

We have been touching in this chapter on the contemplative side of theology. It has not been the predominant aspect in the Western tradition, which has, in McGilchrist's terms, been increasingly dominated by the sort of seeing, thinking and desiring that has characterized the left hemisphere of the brain: grasping, analysing and seeking to control.

---

11   While I would like to be able to take credit for this important insight it is one that I derived from reading Jill Scott's *A Poetics of Forgiveness: Cultural Responses to Loss and Wrongdoing* (New York, Palgrave Macmillan, 2010).

It seems inevitable to me that theology is going to be increasingly contemplative in the future, and that the visual and the poetic will become ever more important to theologians. Among the factors that I believe will push this process along will be our increasingly broad, sophisticated and sympathetic understanding of the beliefs and claims of other religious systems and an ever clearer understanding that a merely 'scientific' approach to life, while splendid at forging breakthroughs in understanding that translate into astonishing applications in terms of technology and medicine, do not actually answer all our questions or deliver the sort of long-term answers and perspectives that satisfy our deepest longings. To deal adequately with those issues we need to engage with something that can properly be called 'theology' and for theology to be itself it must not only be wise enough to learn from its own great history of reflection but bold enough to engage with the realities that press upon people in today's world. Moreover, it must be a discipline that uses to the full the intellectual capacities of the whole human brain, and neither disparages nor fears the power of imagination and imagery or the poetic uses of language.

Such a theology, as well as being a subject open to people of all faiths and none, would have a very broad range of concerns and methods, and these would have to include taking a step beyond even the wider reaches of the fully functioning right cerebral hemisphere and consider the many issues that arise when we begin to take on board the reality that increasing numbers of people are living lives in which brain damage or disease means that they no longer have the capacity even to remember who they are. In the next chapter we consider, among other things, the theological approach to dementia. So please do read on.

CHAPTER 10

THE COMPANY OF THEOLOGIANS

If pressed, I would say that the thing I have enjoyed most about engaging with theology over the years is the company. It was truly astonishing to me when I first heard about and then read in Augustine's *Confessions* that he had framed, pondered and lived with some of the very issues that had long bugged me. Issues such as the kind of thing a person is, how we might come to a view about the existence of God and, if it is positive, how we might relate to the God whom we now believe to exist, and whether and how we might get satisfying answers to eternal questions.

As a former psychologist reading the *Confessions* I was intrigued to notice that Augustine was concerned about the related areas of time and memory. The treatment he gives them is philosophically informed but, as one commentator puts it, the questions that drive him are 'less philosophical than religious'. Certainly he wants to get a profound and precise understanding of the truth about time. For instance, he asks whether or not the past and the future are properly considered to be time. His conclusion is that they are not. Only the present is actually time. The past and the future exist to the extent to which they are called to mind in the present. He is also much concerned about the relationship between the succession of time that we experience and the 'simultaneity of eternity', recognizing that such questions are caught up with the issue of how God created time and space. But with equal urgency Augustine wants to know what sense can be made of the apparent chaos of successive events of personal life and wider history. And it is this question of making sense of life, especially when life does not intuitively seem to 'add up', or to make the sort of sense with which we are comfortable, that can continue to drive the theological quest today. We can understand that Augustine might well have found a theological agenda when he began to think about time and memory; the issues he raises can still make us scratch our heads. But today we might be more inclined to be prompted by theological reflection when we think about the way we *feel* about time, or how we experience it, in particular if we feel that it is running out, or too short, or speeding up or whatever – and the issues that arise not when we remember, but when we forget. The guilty conscience, the sense of sin, the burden of feeling unworthy – this family of feelings has for many centuries had a huge impact on the way in which people have framed their theological questions. And to the extent to which people are able to be disappointed in themselves they will remain part of the theological picture. But as we have already seen, the agenda is broadening out in many ways, and one particularly interesting and significant issue that is beginning to attract the attention of theologians is not the phenomenon of memory but the *loss* of memory caused by brain disease or damage. I am talking here about dementia.

In today's world there is an unprecedented epidemic of people suffering from Alzheimer's disease and the various other conditions which cause dementia. If you look at the graphs showing the increase in usage of the word 'dementia' in books published in English since 1980, you will notice that the curve is comparable to that showing the economic growth of China over the same period. We can think of dementia as a disease, and there are plenty of scientists researching it to find its causes and if possible find ways to arrest its progress or find methods to prevent it developing or cure people of it. But because questions of time, memory, mind and identity are deeply interconnected it is also possible to begin to imagine a theology of dementia.

John Swinton explores the many twists and turns of the questions raised by the Alzheimer's epidemic in a recent book.[1] In it, he argues that a person is still a person even if they lose their mind or have lost all their memories. This is a profoundly important argument ethically, socially and personally. Ethically because it provides a new framework for thinking about the questions of how we might appropriately regard and treat people with advanced dementia, socially because it informs the way in which we might actually relate to people with dementia ourselves, and personally because none of us knows whether we ourselves will one day be living without the cognitive apparatus that is today so important not only to our functioning and flourishing, but also to our sense of who we are. Many people today are frightened of this prospect, and yet the situation presses home on us most profoundly not when we alarm ourselves with the question 'How will I feel when I can no longer remember?' or even, 'Who will I be when I no longer think as I do now?' but when we are challenged to know how to feel about, and relate to, loved ones who find themselves in the grip of some form of neural degeneration while we observe from a positon of clear-eyed and acute-minded despair.

Is it enough to look at dementia from a medical perspective and to describe the biology of the disease and its cognitive

---

1   John Swinton, *Dementia: Living in the Memories of God* (London, SCM Press, 2012).

consequences as a kind of death in life, and to see a living person as a 'hollowed out shell'? Or is it more helpful, realistic and true to say that who we are is only *partly* defined by what we think and remember, and that even in a chronically unreflective state we are fundamentally the person we always were?

As this book has a personal side to it let me come clean on this. As I write this my mother is progressing down the slippery Alzheimer's slope at an alarming pace. It is inevitable that my siblings and I feel that we are losing her. And yet I am not content for the question of who my mother is to be determined by what she *thinks* and *remembers*. There may be a day when she will not know who I am, but it doesn't seem to me a foregone conclusion that she will not at that stage still love me, or that I will no longer be able to love her. Quite how I will relate to her is a different and difficult matter. One thing that bugs me particularly is the question of whether or not it will be 'worth' visiting her if there is no obvious recognition or possibility of meaningful conversation. And alongside this is the question of how I feel about her if I don't visit her. And for that matter how I would end up feeling about myself, my priorities, my values, and my life as a whole if I simply get on with other matters while she subsists in bewildered, mindless confusion cared for by strangers. Yet even as I write this I realize with sadness that even if I were with her as her primary carer she would still be subsisting in bewildered, mindless confusion cared for by strangers – as she would not *know* who I was.

I am not alone in worrying about this, but it is clear to me that it is important to worry about this in a way that is as honest and wise as possible, and that my own worrying about it should therefore be informed by how I think about this as a theologian.

And that thinking is now itself shaped and influenced by the way in which John Swinton has written about it in his book. As well as informing me about many aspects of dementia, and introducing me to a wide literature on the subject and related areas, Swinton has persuaded me that a person is not only what they think they are on the inside, but what their community makes of them from the outside. He has also reminded me of something I have long felt to be true on the basis of my own experience of being with people with dementia, or stroke victims who have lost the powers of speech. Namely, that there are forms of communication that are more than verbal. One might call these 'communing' or simply 'being with'. And Swinton has encouraged me to take the view that just as the mind is more than the brain, so the heart is more than the mind. This has helped me come to appreciate that when I think about my mother it is not her *mind* that I love but her heart or, if you prefer, her soul. And by heart or soul I don't mean some particular aspect of her person, but the wholeness of who she is, or to be precise, the wholeness of her as *I* have experienced and known it over the years. This is the mother I know and love. It is a relationship not entirely dependent on her state of mind or awareness of what is going on now.

It may be crushingly banal to say that a son loves his mother, or vice versa. But to say that a son loves his mother who has advanced dementia and believes that she also loves him even though she doesn't recognize him is to say something that has more radical substance. It means that there is more to life, more to love, more to relationships than we might ordinarily recognize. And what is of interest theologically lies in the realm of that nebulous but vital *more*.

Such are the sort of theological reflections that arise when the metaphysical side of theology comes to the fore in an all too realistic situation. But theology doesn't only look to the beyond, it also looks to the material and the mundane. At the physical, as opposed to the metaphysical level, the reality of dementia triggers theological questions about the significance of bodily life. It is not the only reality to trigger such questions, of course, but I mention in passing that no one seriously considers a preverbal infant to be a 'shell' or difficult to love. Indeed, being unable to love a baby is seen as a kind of pathology. Loving babies is natural, instant and easy. We know ourselves to be hard-wired to do this and the evolutionary psychologists will tell us why. But the theologian is one who always declines to be satisfied with reductionist answers to life's deepest questions. It's simply not interesting or important enough to say that's just the way we have evolved. The theologian is interested in the *meaning* of the life of a person with dementia, not just its 'quality'. The preverbal infant may be valued because of their charm and potential, but the post-verbal person can be valued for their past, not understood as a reservoir of experience that might be applied in the present or future but through the memories and loves of others.

This doesn't make a theologian antagonistic towards scientific or medical perspectives. The point rather is that they will be concerned to push the horizon of meaning and purpose back, and to consider the bigger picture, the deeper issues, the longer-term perspective – the eternal questions. A theologian will always want to be in the realm of 'science plus'. As Swinton rightly argues at the beginning of his book, the theologian should not settle for the approach that allows science or medicine to set the terms of the discussion, or provide the predominant or exclusive lens though which issues are viewed, or set the rules within which discussions are held or life-and-death decisions made. This is often the way it goes, however, and it is exacerbated in the modern world by the way in which people often resort to religious thinking, or seek 'spiritual help', only when all other forms have either evaporated or been found wanting. A theologian can't be entirely happy with this state of affairs, although neither will a theologian be surprised if issues and questions arise that are beyond the range of competence and experience of practitioners, professionals and thinkers who limit themselves to the certainly knowable. Limited thinking is always going to find itself, well, limited.

The theologian will argue that questions of meaning, value, purpose need to be considered in the context not only of evidence but of the traditions of discussion and debate that have developed in different cultures over the centuries. The theologian, the dealer in eternal questions, will never be satisfied with the realm of the definitively knowable. Whether a committed believer or an enquiring agnostic, they will constantly question where the ultimate horizon lies and seek to ask the most significant questions about meaning and purpose, love and hope; all the while recognizing that these are both extremely difficult and fundamentally ordinary questions, and that they are both the first and the last things for us to think about.

Reflecting on the implications of dementia seems like a very contemporary and modern thing to do – consider again that growth curve which rivals the economic development of China. And yet the point about looking at this theologically is that you are looking in a way that has the deepest of historical as well as philosophical roots, and which refuses to go down the all too convenient, and controlling, reductionist path.

A COMMUNITY OF QUESTIONERS

When I talk about the company of theologians I don't primarily refer to the people who teach theology at universities or those who write learned books, but to the whole community of people who dare to articulate the troubling questions of meaning and purpose; those who, when they feel the pain of existence in a personal tragedy or natural disaster, don't just shrug their shoulders or turn back to their latest pastime, but allow the question 'Why?' to surface, and then seek with patient wisdom to assuage some of its agonized fury with answers that are potentially worthy of the question. Poets and artists are among those who enter into the theological arena, but so too are those who discover within themselves the kind of existential determination that makes them want to care about people whom others reject or pass by, or to love those who are not easy to love, and to remain faithful to those who so change in the course of their lives that they can no longer sustain their own identity from within. We have already seen that theology ultimately invites us to engage in a way of thinking and being that is contemplative and not dominated by verbal categories or anxious analysis. As we come to the end of this book we also see that theology needs to be consistent with its own core value and purpose. This is where the word 'love' raises its uniquely important head once again.

To explore theology, to try to communicate meaningfully while using the word God, involves an exploration of love – both the word 'love' and the reality of love. 'Love bade me welcome,' wrote George Herbert in the poem I quoted in the tweets chapter. On the other hand, there is no time at which Love bids me, or you, farewell. And this is one of the reasons why theology is endless. There may come a day when restless God-curiosity modulates into in a contented contemplation that calms – Augustine's sense that restlessness can be satisfied; but this calm will not be the end of God-curiosity. Rather it is a different, more mature and settled form. Augustine was, after all, most productive only once his heart was cured of its restlessness.

Theology may never be able precisely to define God, or to prove the existence of God, but it must always take the question of God seriously. And that is not just the question of whether or not God exists but also the question of what God is like. For the tradition which I inherit and try to inhabit a fundamental issue concerns the nature of God as love. It is this proposition – God is love – that the Christian tradition, while as diverse and varied as you can imagine on most subjects, is in agreement. And, love being love, it is simultaneously thought and feeling, and always a stimulus for both reflection and action.

Ultimately, then, Christian theology is an extended meditation on the nature and implications of the belief that God exists, is love, and that the loving creator, who is also, in Elizabeth Johnson's terms, the Creator Spirit, is not only the first and last reality, but also both utterly transcendent and infinitely close. It is this sort of theology that insists, with liberation theologian Gustavo Gutierrez, that there is no distinction between sacred and secular, but that history is one, and that therefore there is no realm of experience or enquiry which is intrinsically beyond the borders of theological questioning. This is also the sort of theology that emphasizes our common creatureliness, our *kinship*, ahead of our cognitive capacities, our personal will or anything else that makes us singular and individual rather than communal and connected. Or at least, that is Christian theology from this practitioner's perspective.

Engaging with eternal questions in the way that I have been promoting in these pages is something open to believers and atheists provided that they have a modest degree of what one might think of as small-a agnosticism. This is the inquisitive and exploratory spirit of the God-curious. Its mode of thought is likely to be 'I'm not really sure about that,' or 'Come to think of it, I am uncertain about how to engage with this issue, but I have a feeling that the apparent consensus is not quite right.' Small-a agnosticism is open not only to the unexpected, but also to the unanswerable question, which it doesn't seek to answer quickly but to open up slowly. It is prepared to explore questions of faith and has the confidence to live with, and even find benefit in, uncertainty. The God-curious, whether believer or atheist, must be prepared to move away from the confident certainty that they have already got these matters tidied up and sorted out to an entirely adequate degree if they are to engage with theology, if they are to grow in wisdom through their God-curiosity.

The atheist with a quotient of small-a agnosticism will stand aside from the belief that love is the ultimate reality and the conviction expressed by Julian of Norwich that 'all shall be well, and all shall be well and all manner of thing shall be well'. But the atheist theologian will be just as distant from the not so subtle shortcuts of materialistic reductionism, the apparently endless mission-creep of scientific method and the inbuilt control-freakery of rational thinking, and will endlessly enquire into the possibility that wisdom might be found in religious belief or practice or in theological formulations of theoretical and practical problems. Some atheists will welcome the company of theologians from the faith traditions to help strengthen a conspiracy against fundamentalism and the wrong sort of dogmatism and narrow-minded foreclosing of questions about deep and important issues. Some, for instance, will not easily want to think of a parent or sibling as a hollowed-out, meaningless shell because they have seen a brain scan and can no longer even have a conversation about happy holidays long ago, but will be relatively comfortable with sitting in the cloudy silence of unknowing.

To attempt to speak out of such silence about what might be going on beyond the evidently known is the effort and practice of theology, whether or not the theologian is a person of faith or an atheist. It is always a journey of exploration and sometimes one of discovery. It requires a mixture of curiosity, humility, patience and determination, and a willingness to engage in some way with the wide and diverse, historical and contemporary, company of theologians – those who ask the eternal questions with persistence and seriousness.

There are no limits regarding when you might embark on such a journey. Nor are there any rules about the direction in which you might travel, or the means by which you make progress.

There are extensive, wonderful and diverse resources to help you on your way. Among these are the traditions of theology in the past, and all the people who have in many different ways lived with, and sought to pose and answer theological questions, and then pose some more.

In these pages you have briefly met some of the great theologians of the past: people who have given extensive time and energy to this same process of exploration. You have learnt both from the way in which they see the issues and the way in which they tried to make some progress by making positive statements and by engaging in debate. Below the surface of the statements and the questions there is the less visible discipline of reflective attention, which I have tried to bring into focus both by thinking about art and poetry and the awful reality of dementia. These are questions that are both fresh and, at a deeper level, not so different to the sorts of questions that have been spurring and shaping theology for centuries.

I hope that some of the theologians mentioned will become your companions, and that you will be inspired to continue the exploration in the way that works best for you given your personality, your age, your education, your religious inheritance and your personal faith – or lack of faith. There is no need to travel alone; just as God is understood to be love, so faith is deeply connected with relationship and community. You can find the company of theologians not only in the great books of the past but also in the presence of those who have the courage and patience to live openly with challenging, fundamental and eternal questions today.

For some this might mean studying theology at university. It's a tremendous subject and in most universities there is a very wide range of options so you can genuinely explore in a way that challenges you and equips you for life as a graduate. For others it might involve joining a course set up by a local religious community, or maybe visiting the religious section of museums, or watching movies or reading novels with religious themes, or getting the local library to stock up on some of the theological classics, or even buying the books of contemporary theologians as they come out. There are very many ways of exploring theology – the key to them all is to recognize your God-curiosity and to give it some time, space and energy.

Don't let this be the end of your theological exploring; let it be the beginning – as well as being great fun it could become the most fascinating and important part of your life. Go well, and may you be both humbled and enriched as you pursue your God-curiosity wherever it leads.

ACKNOWLEDGEMENTS

As this book touches on things that I have learnt over the whole course of my adult life the list of all those whose insights, generosity and wisdom have helped me along the way would be very lengthy and, given the human capacity to forget or fail to appreciate fully, incomplete. Let me rather mention those who have been particularly helpful and kind in commenting on and responding to drafts of this book: Luke Stephen, Karenza Passmore and James Cherry. It has been a real delight to work with Jessica Kingsley, and I am especially grateful for her immediate and generous enthusiasm for the project and the kindly editorial suggestions and questions that were such an important part of the creative process of writing this book.